THE

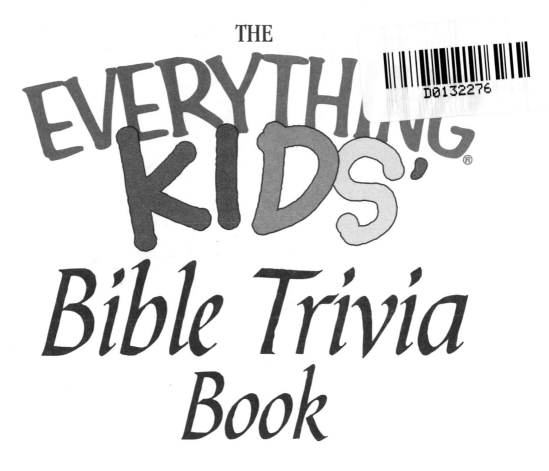

EVERYTHING KIDS'

Bible Trivia Book

Stump your friends and family
with your Bible knowledge!

Kathi Wagner and Aubrey Wagner

Adams Media
Avon, Massachusetts

To God who knows. To Barb and Bob Doyen for believing in us.
To the Stuarts, who have reminded me how enjoyable it can be.
—Aubrey Wagner

EDITORIAL
Publishing Director: Gary M. Krebs
Managing Editor: Kate McBride
Copy Chief: Laura MacLaughlin
Acquisitions Editor: Bethany Brown
Development Editor: Julie Gutin
Production Editor: Jamie Wielgus

PRODUCTION
Production Director: Susan Beale
Production Manager: Michelle Roy Kelly
Series Designer: Colleen Cunningham
Layout and Graphics: Paul Beatrice, Colleen
Cunningham, Rachael Eiben, John Paulhus,
Daria Perreault, Erin Ring, Frank Rivera

An *Everything*® Series Book.
Everything® and everything.com® are registered trademarks of F+W Publications, Inc.

Published by Adams Media, an F+W Publications Company
57 Littlefield Street, Avon, MA 02322 U.S.A.
www.adamsmedia.com

ISBN: 1-59337-031-8

Printed in the United States of America.

J I H G F E D C B A

This publication is designed to provide accurate and authoritative information with regard to the subject
matter covered. It is sold with the understanding that the publisher is not engaged in rendering legal,
accounting, or other professional advice. If legal advice or other expert assistance is required, the services of
a competent professional person should be sought.
— From a *Declaration of Principles* jointly adopted
by a Committee of the American Bar Association and a Committee of Publishers and Associations

Many of the designations used by manufacturers and sellers to distinguish their products are claimed as
trademarks. Where those designations appear in this book and Adams Media was aware of a trademark
claim, the designations have been printed in initial capital letters.

Cover illustrations by Dana Regan.
Interior illustrations by Kurt Dolber.
Puzzles by Beth Blair.

Puzzle Power Software by Centron Software Technologies, Inc. was used to create some puzzle grids.

This book is available at quantity discounts for bulk purchases.
For information, call 1-800-872-5627.

See the entire Everything® series at *www.everything.com*.

Contents

Introduction / v

Introduction

Almost everyone has heard of the Bible or knows something about God. This is probably due to the fact that no other book has ever been more available, no matter where you live, what language you speak, or even the type of faith you have. The word *Bible* comes from a Greek word meaning *books*. Never has a book had a more fitting title. Not only is the Bible a book in itself, but it is also a collection of several smaller books—books that speak of angels and miracles, spirits and visions, of people and of God.

Not surprisingly, the Bible has set almost every record possible for a book. The fact that it has remained popular from the first day it was written is a good place to start. To that you can add its record for the most copies sold, translated, and shared throughout the world. Not to mention the record 1,000 years that it took to write it.

With God as the author, it took the work of approximately fifty scribes or message writers to record the Holy Scriptures. In Biblical times there were no printers or photocopiers. The only way you could have your own volume of the Bible would be to have someone copy all of the words down for you by hand. Many felt the message God had to share, a message of faith and love and forgiveness and salvation (being saved), was worth the time it took to record it.

Everything about the Bible is rare. This one of a kind book speaks of the past, the present, and the future. No other book of its time explained in such detail the history and the law of the land, as well as all of the unusual events that were taking place. Throughout the ages, some people have thought the Bible may have been written as a story to entertain. Yet, when these people try to prove that the Bible is wrong or fake, the opposite usually happens. In their attempt to find error, they actually find that many of the events and places that are recorded in the pages of the Scriptures have happened and do really exist.

Although there are many different types of bibles, some that have more or less books inside of them, the one thing all bibles agree on is the message of God's love. This message appears in the first half of the Bible, known as the Old Testament, which tells about God's world. And it's also in the second half—the New Testament—which speaks of God's son. One of the promises God made in the Bible was to share the Good News or Word with others. Billions of copies of this promise have made their way into our homes and churches alike. Many religions use the Bible to teach others about God and love. One can only guess how important the Bible has been to our world, and the effect its words have had on us—words that keep asking us to be kind to each other, and to try to get along.

Acknowledgments

We would like to thank Sheryl Racine for her constant support and help. There has never been a better researcher, proofreader, mother, or grandmother.

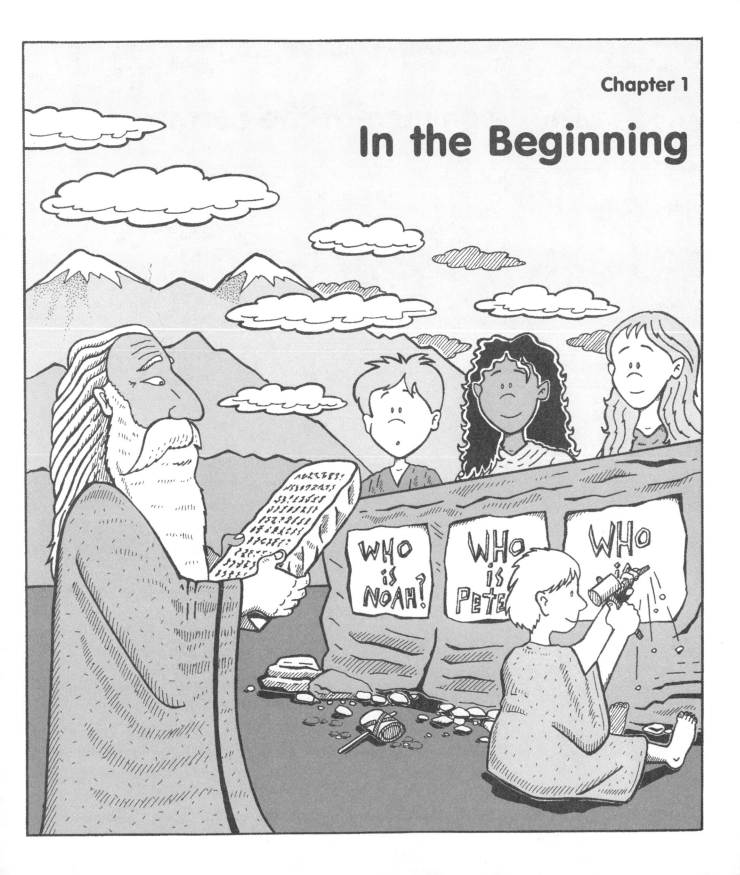

In the Beginning

The Beginning of the Earth

religion: A belief in the creator of the universe. It is also a study or practice of faith in a god and the rules given to Man. There are Many different religions or faiths in our world.

Words to Know

Fun Fact

That's Old!

If you were born during the time when the Bible was written you could have had as many as 900 candles on your cake. Not to mention more than 900 parties, and all of those presents!

1. What day did God pick to rest on after creating the heavens and the Earth?

2. What was another name for *darkness*?
   a. Night
   b. Evil
   c. Cold
   d. The end

3. What lights did God create on the fourth day?

4. On which day were the creatures of the waters made?
   a. The fifth day
   b. The sixth day
   c. The seventh day
   d. The fourth day

5. Do you know what God made to mark the seasons?

6. In the beginning, what was on the face of the Earth?
   a. Mountains
   b. People
   c. Darkness
   d. Serpents

7. On what day were trees created?

8. Whose spirit was hovering over the waters?

9. What were the winged creatures God made on the fifth day?
   a. Bats
   b. Butterflies
   c. Birds
   d. Pterodactyls

10. On which day did God also create the stars?
    a. The fourth day
    b. The fifth day
    c. The third day
    d. The sixth day

11. What were the waters called when they were gathered together?

12. God used another name for light—what was it?

Amazing Creation

Find your way through all of God's creation, STARTing on the first day
and winding around until the seventh day, when He RESTed.

The First Man

Who Am I?

When the world was very young, I was quite old. In my life I lived to be 910 years of age. When I was seventy, I became the father of Mahalalel. **Who am I?**

Kenan

1. What does the word *image* mean?
   a. How old you are
   b. What you know
   c. What you look like
   d. How you think

2. Do you know what the first man ruled over in the air?
   a. Airplanes
   b. Winds
   c. Insects
   d. Birds

3. Did God want man to increase or decrease?

4. What kind of plant did God give to man?

5. Why did God give man fruits with seeds in them?

6. What color of plant did God say was for food?
   a. Brown   c. Red
   b. Green   d. Yellow

7. How were the plants in the ground watered?

8. Where could one find gold at this time?

9. What was the name of the third river that God spoke of?
   a. Pishon
   b. Gihon
   c. Tigris
   d. Euphrates

10. Asshur was located in Assyria in the time of the Bible. What do we call that country now?

11. What happened to Adam when God breathed into him?

12. God enjoyed trees for more than just their fruit. What was the other reason?

A Message for You

Angels are sometimes called the messengers of God. In the Bible angels were sent to guide or watch over people. Many times God sent an angel to carry His words from Heaven to Earth.

Fun Fact

After the Lord God made man, He realized it was not good for man to be alone. —Genesis 2:18–25

A Wedding

1. When a man marries, whom does he leave?

2. What did Adam need most of all in the world?
   a. A gardener
   b. A helper
   c. Money
   d. A new house

3. To whom is a man united in marriage?

4. What did God cause Adam to fall into?
   a. A well   c. A river
   b. A hole   d. A deep sleep

5. What did God take away from Adam?

6. What did God do with Adam's rib?

7. After God made the woman what did He do?

8. Why was this new creation called *woman*?

9. How did Adam finish this sentence? "This is now bone of my . . ."
   a. Flesh   c. Father
   b. Bones   d. Body

10. In a marriage, two become what?
    a. One   c. More
    b. A family d. Two

Bible: The Bible is the Word of God that is held sacred in Christianity and Judaism. In this book you will find psalms, songs, history, and rules created to teach man about life in the past, present, and future.

Words to Know

TRY THIS

▶ *A Taste Test*

Can you tell what fruit you are eating if you have a blindfold on? What if the fruits are similar such as a piece of lemon, a piece of lime, and a piece of grapefruit? Would you be able to tell the difference? There is only one sure way to find out—you'll have to take a taste test!

The Tree of Knowledge

1. Which animal in the Garden was considered to be the craftiest?
   a. The serpent
   b. The fox
   c. The weasel
   d. The cat

2. What did God tell Adam and Eve that they could eat?
   a. They couldn't eat anything
   b. Only the oranges
   c. All of the fruits in the Garden
   d. Everything but the fruit of the tree of knowledge

3. Whose idea was it for Eve to try the first bite?

4. Where was the tree of knowledge located in the Garden?
   a. In the back
   b. In the middle
   c. By the gate
   d. In the front

5. Did the snake believe that Adam and Eve could not eat the fruit?

6. What did God say would happen if they touched the fruit?

7. When Adam and Eve ate the apple, what happened?

8. When Adam and Eve finished eating the fruit of knowledge, what did they do next?
   a. They read
   b. They followed the serpent
   c. They slept
   d. They sewed together fig leaves to cover themselves

9. Where was God when He discovered the truth about Adam and Eve?

10. Why were they hiding?

11. When God asked who was to blame, what did Adam say?

12. Who did Eve blame for all of the trouble?

Applesauce

To make applesauce, you need: 4 apples, ½ cup water, and ¼ cup sugar. To start, wash your apples. Next, ask an adult to cut them in fourths, peel them, and remove the seeds. Now you are ready to boil the apples in a pan of water. Once the water begins to boil, place a lid on top and turn down the heat to a simmer. After 20 minutes, your apples are done and ready to cool. Then you can mash them with a fork, add the sugar, and eat.

Find the Snake

Can you find where the sneaky snake is hiding in this Garden of Eden?
HINT: He's right next to the one time in this puzzle where the word APPLE is spelled correctly.

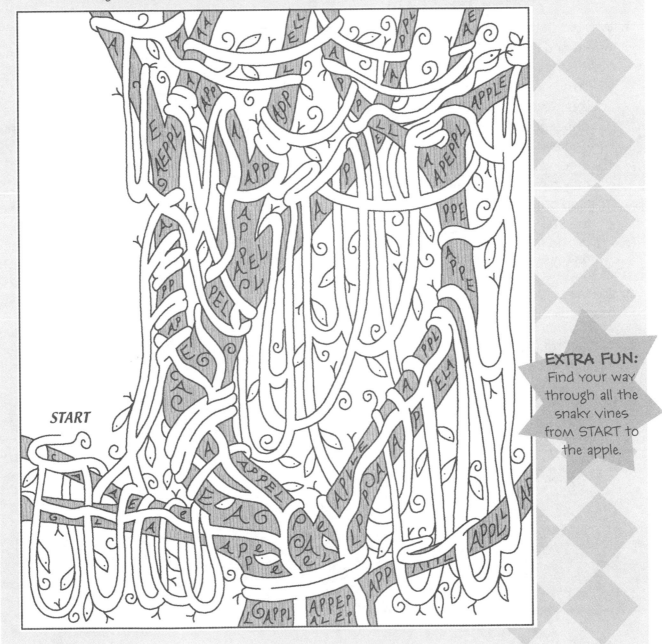

START

EXTRA FUN: Find your way through all the snaky vines from START to the apple.

The Move

1. Why did God try to warn Adam and Eve about the tree? He knew the tree would:
   a. Teach them about good and evil
   b. Break when they climbed it
   c. Stop growing if the fruit was picked too soon
   d. Be poisonous

2. Did the serpent really mean to cause trouble?

3. Who took the first bite of the apple?
   a. The serpent   c. Adam
   b. Eve   d. God

4. How did God punish the serpent for what he did?

5. Who gave Eve her name, Adam or God?

6. The knowledge Adam and Eve got from the tree made them feel shame for not wearing what?
   a. Hats   c. Gloves
   b. Coats   d. Clothes

7. What were Adam and Eve's first clothes?

8. Later God gave them clothes to wear. What were they made of?

9. What does God tell Adam his fields will produce?
   a. Thorns and thistles
   b. Crops of gold
   c. Prize harvests
   d. Food for the thousands

10. What did God use to keep Adam and Eve from returning to the Garden of Eden?

11. What did God tell the serpent he would eat for the rest of his days?

Hard to Swallow

Adam's apple is a nickname that has been given to the lump you see on the front of some people's throats. Some believe it is there as a reminder to us of the original piece of the apple that Adam ate.

Fun Fact

A New Baby

1. What was the name of Adam and Eve's first son?

2. What did they name their second son?
   a. Shem   c. Cush
   b. Abel   d. Lemech

3. What type of work did their firstborn son do?

4. What type of work did their second son do?
   a. He was a carpenter
   b. He was a priest
   c. He was a ship builder
   d. He was a shepherd

5. What offering did the second son make to the Lord?

6. Whose offering did the Lord prefer?

7. When the Lord asked Cain, "Why is your face downcast?" what did He mean?
   a. "Why do you look upset?"
   b. "Why is your face looking down?"
   c. "Why do you look down on me?"
   d. "Why do you look happy?"

8. Did the two brothers get along?

9. When Cain asked the Lord, "Am I my brother's keeper?" what did he mean?

10. How did the Lord know something had happened to Abel?

11. What did the Lord do to punish Cain for hurting his brother?

12. Why did the Lord mark Cain?

Who Am I?

Sometimes you see me, yet sometimes you don't. Even when you do not see me, I am still there. I am a father and I am a son. **Who am I?**

God

birthright: In the days of the Bible it allowed the oldest son to inherit or receive everything that his father had. Some places in the world today still practice or honor the birthright.

Words to Know

Why couldn't Cain please God with his offering?

He just wasn't Abel!

Where do kids go for recess after church?

The pray-ground!

The Land of Nod

1. Where is the land of Nod?

2. What was the name of Cain's first son?

3. What else was Enoch a name for?
   a. A drink   c. Food
   b. A city   d. A river

4. Who was Cain's great-great-great-grandson?

5. What instruments did Lamech's son Jubal play?
   a. The harp and the flute
   b. The trumpet and the horn
   c. The lyre and the cymbals
   d. The bells and the harp

6. What would be God's penalty to anyone who tried to harm Cain?

7. When Adam and Eve had a third son, what did they name him?

8. Who was Adam and Eve's third son's son?

9. How old did many of the men from the Bible live to be?
   a. 100 years old
   b. 200 years old
   c. 900 years old
   d. 400 years old

10. What do you call the average time between the birth of parents and their children, grandchildren, and great-grandchildren?

The Dead Sea Library

The Dead Sea Scrolls are ancient texts written on rolls of leather and papyrus. They are some of the first books found in one of the first libraries. The Bible was one of the books found in the caves.

Fun Fact

Father to Son

1. Who was Noah? Was he Methuselah's:
   a. Son
   b. Grandson
   c. Great-grandson
   d. Brother

2. Who was Lamech? Was he Noah's:
   a. Grandfather
   b. Father
   c. Son
   d. Grandson

3. Noah had three sons. What were their names?

4. After the birth of Noah's sons, how many years passed before the flood?
   a. Fifty years
   b. Seventy years
   c. Less than 100 years
   d. More than 100 years

5. The Bible describes men of renown. What are they?
   a. Men from the city
   b. Farmers
   c. Famous men
   d. Good men

6. What did Noah find in the eyes of the Lord?

7. When Noah spent time with the Lord did he walk, play, or argue?

Happy Father's Day

Three letters are missing from this list of biblical fathers and sons. Can you fill them in correctly? When you're finished, add up the numbers under each name and write the answer in the white box. This will tell you, according to the Bible, how old each man was when he became a father for the first time!

_ D _ M
13 25 73 19

Adam was the father of
E T H
27 19 32 27

Seth was the father of
E N O _ H
9 53 12 3 13

Enosh was the father of
K E N _ N
5 37 17 6 5

Kenan was the father of
M _ H _ L _ L E L
12 3 4 10 12 13 3 1 7

Mahalalel was the father of
J _ R E D
30 31 30 31 40

Jared was the father of
E N O _ H
13 13 13 13 13

Enoch was the father of
M E T H U _ E L _ H
15 9 8 7 9 8 7 9 8 7

Methuselah was the father of
L _ M E _ H
33 22 44 11 55 17

Lamech was the father of
N O _ H
125 100 125 150

Chapter 1 Answer Key

The Beginning of the Earth
1. The seventh day
2. a. Night
3. The sun and moon
4. a. The fifth day
5. The lights
6. c. Darkness
7. The third day
8. God's spirit
9. c. Birds
10. a. The fourth day
11. Seas
12. Day

The First Man
1. c. What you look like
2. d. Birds
3. Increase
4. The seed-bearing type
5. For food
6. b. Green
7. By streams from the ground
8. In Havilah
9. c. Tigris
10. Iraq
11. He became a living being
12. They were pleasing to the eye

A Wedding
1. His father and mother
2. b. A helper
3. His wife
4. A deep sleep
5. His rib
6. He made a woman
7. He brought her to Adam
8. She was taken out of man
9. b. Bones
10. a. One

The Tree of Knowledge
1. a. The serpent
2. d. Everything but the fruit of the tree of knowledge
3. The serpent's
4. b. In the middle
5. No
6. That they would die
7. Their eyes were opened to new knowledge
8. d. They sewed together fig leaves to cover themselves
9. Walking in the garden
10. Because they were afraid
11. That Eve was to blame
12. The serpent

The Move
1. a. Teach them about good and evil
2. Yes
3. b. Eve
4. He made it crawl on its belly
5. Adam named her
6. d. Clothes
7. Fig leaves
8. Animal skins
9. a. Thorns and thistles
10. A flaming sword
11. Dust

A New Baby
1. Cain
2. b. Abel
3. He was a farmer
4. d. He was a shepherd
5. Parts of a firstborn sheep
6. Abel's
7. a. "Why do you look upset?"
8. No
9. He was asking if it was his job to keep track of his brother
10. He heard a cry
11. He made Cain wander the Earth
12. To keep him safe from others

The Land of Nod
1. East of the Garden of Eden
2. Enoch
3. b. A city
4. Lamech
5. a. The harp and the flute
6. The culprit will be punished seven times
7. Seth
8. Enosh
9. c. 900 years old
10. Generations

Father to Son
1. b. Grandson
2. b. Father
3. Shem, Ham, and Japheth
4. c. Less than 100 years
5. c. Famous men
6. Favor
7. He walked with the Lord

Travel by Ark

1. How long was the ark supposed to be?

2. What kind of wood was used to make the ark?
   a. Cypress
   b. Cedar
   c. Pine
   d. Oak

3. How wide did God instruct Noah to make the ark?

4. What was the ark coated with?
   a. Paint
   b. Gum from the gum tree
   c. Mud
   d. Pitch

5. Did the ark have a roof?

6. When the Lord spoke of destroying the Earth, what did he say would destroy it?

7. When God established a *covenant* with Noah, what did that mean?

8. What kind of food did Noah bring?
   a. Food that wouldn't spoil
   b. Every kind
   c. Fresh food
   d. He didn't bring any food

9. Who were the people God allowed Noah to bring into the ark with him?

10. How many doors were in the ark?

11. What else did God tell Noah to bring onto the ark?

12. How many levels did the ark have?
    a. One
    b. Two
    c. Three
    d. Four

Edible Ark Animals

Edible ark animals are easy to make and fun to eat. All you need are a few foods that were actually around at the time of the Bible—cucumbers, olives, carrots, raisins, cheese, and other vegetables and garnishes. After washing the vegetables, take your cucumber and using toothpicks add olive eyes, a carrot nose, raisin ears, cheese for fur, and so on. Use your imagination to sculpt any animal you like. After you're done creating, you can eat your veggie-animal with salad dressing.

God must decide which creatures will be saved during and after the flood. —Genesis 7:1–8:22

Two by Two

1. How many of each kind of animal was taken into the ark?

2. God describes some of the animals as *unclean*. True or false?

3. How many days and nights did it rain?

4. What mountain did the ark come to rest on?

5. Where is that mountain located?
   a. In Israel
   b. In Egypt
   c. In Turkey
   d. In Greece

6. What was the first bird that Noah sent out from the ark?

7. Which bird did Noah send out next?
   a. A hawk
   b. An owl
   c. A raven
   d. A dove

8. When the second bird returned to the ark, what did it bring back?

9. What was the first thing Noah did after he came out of the ark?

10. Which of the following animals is a fowl?
    a. A goose
    b. A goat
    c. A tiger
    d. A fox

11. Which animal would not be considered a creeping thing?
    a. A centipede
    b. A serpent
    c. A worm
    d. A horse

12. How long did Noah, his family, and all the animals live in the ark?

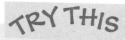

TRY THIS

▶ A Rainbow in a Drinking Glass

Have you ever made a rainbow in a drinking glass? You can if you have one clear drinking glass and three bowls of chilled gelatin—one red, one blue, and one yellow. To make a rainbow, place a few spoonfuls of blue on the bottom, yellow in the middle, and red on top; stir gently. If you want a rainbow in the clouds, add some whipped cream.

Fun Fact

It Was a Zoo!

Most people think that the ark held only two of each animal. When Noah loaded the boat he did add two of each kind, but he also added five more of each clean animal, making a total of seven of each clean variety.

Two by Two

The ark needed to carry two of every kind of animal, as well as Noah, his wife, his sons, and their wives, too! Follow these directions and you will see how crowded the ark might have been.

1. Find box 1-A and copy it into square 1-A in the grid.
2. Find box 1-B and copy it into square 1-B in the grid.
3. Continue this process until you've copied all the boxes into the grid.

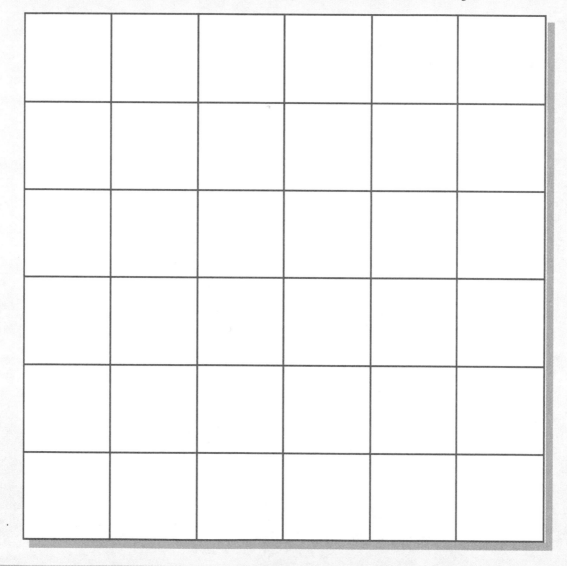

3D   1B   4E   1D   5B   2D

2A   4C   2E   6C   5C   6F

5D   1C   3C   3B   5E   6A

4A   1E   6D   3E   5A   2B

3F   2C   2F   6E   1A   3A

5F   6B   4D   1F   4B   4F

God makes a promise to Noah and his people for all time. —Genesis 9:13–10:32

A Rainbow

1. Who were the people God called Noah's *descendants?*

2. What promise did God make?

3. God said, "I will establish my covenant with you." What's a *covenant?*
   a. A covering
   b. A place
   c. A house
   d. An agreement

4. Do you know what the sign of God's promise to Noah was?

5. What colors do we see in a rainbow?

6. If you combined all the colors of the rainbow, what color would it make?

7. Who was Nimrod, the "mighty hunter before the Lord"?

8. Which one of Noah's sons was the father of Canaan?
   a. Ham
   b. Shem
   c. Japheth

9. Whose sons were the Japhethites?

10. Whom does the Bible call the descendants of Shem?

11. Where did the people of Noah's time live?
    a. In houses
    b. In caves
    c. In castles
    d. In tents

12. Noah was a "man of the soil." What does that mean?
    a. He was married
    b. He was a shepherd
    c. He was a farmer
    d. He was a widow

Two in One

When you look at a rainbow, you may only see a few colors and one bow. But, did you know that there are really two bows? If you look a little closer, you will see the second bow which is the opposite of the first, right above it. Together they contain the following color order: purple, indigo, blue, green, yellow, orange, and red; red, orange, yellow, green, blue, indigo, and purple.

*When God's people try to build a tower and a name of their own,
a displeased Lord makes them unable to work together. —Genesis 11:1–32*

The Tower of Babel

1. At this time, how many languages did the people of the Earth speak?
   a. One language
   b. Three languages
   c. Many languages

2. The Earth divided in the days of Peleg. Who was he?

3. When the Earth *divided*, what did that mean?
   a. The world broke into pieces
   b. The water separated the nations of the world
   c. People began speaking different languages
   d. The dust of the earth blew all around

4. What did the people try to build?
   a. A wall
   b. A tower
   c. A skyscraper
   d. A city

5. What did the people use during the construction?
   a. Straw   c. Wood
   b. Rocks   d. Bricks

6. How tall did they plan to make the building?

7. How did they keep the bricks in place?

8. How did the Lord stop their plan to build the tower?

9. After the people could no longer understand each other, where did the Lord send them?

10. Who was the father of Abram?

Who Am I?

I made a mistake that changed the world. It took only a second, a weak moment, and a few encouraging words from someone else. Now things will never be the same.
Who am I?

Eve

TRY THIS

▶ Blueprints for a Tower

You can build your own tower out of sugar cubes and icing. Draw a circle on a paper plate about five inches wide. Squirt your icing on the circle and begin to lay the sugar cube bricks. After each layer, add some more icing. Keep adding layers one on top of another until you reach the height you want your tower to be.

Abram Follows

anoint: The Bible tells of people who were anointed—marked with special oil. This sacred practice was used after bathing, for religious ceremonies, and for the appointment of people to positions of importance.

Words to Know

1. Whom did Abram choose for a wife?
   a. Ruth
   b. Leah
   c. Sarai
   d. Naomi

2. For a long time, how many children did Sarai have?
   a. No children
   b. Two children
   c. Four children
   d. Six children

3. Where did Abram's father establish their family?

4. The Lord told Abram, "Leave your country, your people, and your father's household and go to the land I will show you." What did the Lord mean by *your people*?
   a. Your relatives
   b. Your belongings
   c. Your neighbors
   d. Your ancestors

5. To whom did the Lord promise the land of Canaan?

6. When they found a famine in Negev, what did they do?

7. What happens during a famine?
   a. People don't have enough to drink
   b. There is a flood
   c. There is a war
   d. People don't have enough to eat

8. Who was the leader of Egypt?
   a. The king
   b. The tsar
   c. The pharaoh
   d. The queen

9. What did the Lord inflict on the Pharaoh?
   a. Lies
   b. Baldness
   c. Curses
   d. Diseases

10. When Abram and Lot began to argue, where did Lot go?

11. What did the Lord mean when He told Abram, "I will make your offspring like the dust of the Earth."

12. How much was the tithe or amount given after Lot's return?

Abram is asked to trust in the Lord. In return, he will be taken care of and rewarded. —Geneses 15:1–11

Do Not Be Afraid

1. The Lord said, "Do not be afraid, Abram. I am your shield." What did He mean?

2. Abram tells the Lord that Eliezer will inherit his estate. What does it mean that he will *inherit* it?
   a. He will serve it
   b. He will manage it
   c. He will leave it
   d. He will sell it

3. What does the word *sovereign* mean?

4. When the Lord speaks to Abram about his *heir*, who or what is He talking about?
   a. His beard
   b. The sky
   c. Someone to inherit what he owns
   d. His best friend

5. God told Abram to "Look up at the heavens" and do what?

6. Why was Abram worried about who would inherit all he had?

7. The Lord asked Abram for a heifer. What is a *heifer*? A young:
   a. Mare   c. Bull
   b. Cow   d. Pig

8. The Lord brought Abram out of Ur of the Chaldees, also known as Mesopotamia, the land between the Tigris and the Euphrates Rivers. What is the name of that country today?
   a. Iraq   c. Egypt
   b. Syria   d. Lebanon

A Beautiful Promise

The letters in each column go in the squares directly below them, but not necessarily in the same order! Black squares are the spaces between words. When you have correctly filled in the grid, you will know the promise that God made to Noah and all the world after the great flood.

EXTRA FUN: Use the clues to help you color in the rainbow, a symbol of God's promise!

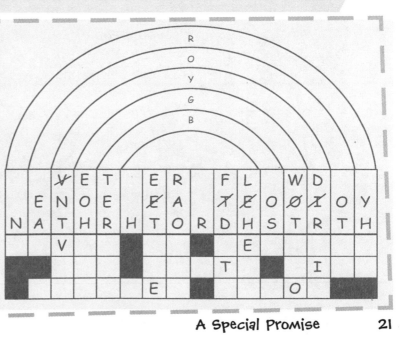

A Special Promise   21

Abram's Dream

1. While Abram slept, what came over him?
   a. Rain from God
   b. A nightmare
   c. A thick and dreadful darkness
   d. Rocks from a cliff

2. Who was the child born to Abram and his second wife Hagar?
   a. Cain   c. Lot
   b. Joseph   d. Ishmael

3. Why did the Lord change Abram's name to Abraham?

4. What name did God give to Abraham's wife Sarai?
   a. Sahara   c. Sarah
   b. Samantha   d. Saraii

5. Why did the Lord establish a covenant with Abraham and his descendants?
   a. To be their friend
   b. To be their neighbor
   c. To be their God
   d. To be their leader

6. Who was the child God promised to Abraham and his wife?

7. Why did the Lord decide to destroy the towns of Sodom and Gomorrah?

8. What happened to Lot's wife when she disobeyed the Lord and looked back at Sodom and Gomorrah?

9. God declared Abraham to be a prophet. What does a prophet do?
   a. Builds temples
   b. Speaks the Word of the Lord
   b. Writes poems
   b. Leads armies

Where does a skunk sit in church?

In a "pew"!

Fun Fact

A New Identity

Did you know that some people change their own name? For a small fee and a little time at a courthouse, anyone can legally change his or her name. Another way to have a name change is through marriage. A wife can take her husband's name or a husband can take his wife's. Many people say they don't like their own name, but when they hear about the other names their parents considered, they almost always prefer the one they have.

With Isaac's birth, Sarah begins to worry about Abraham's loyalty to Ishmael. —Genesis 21:1–34

Isaac Is Born

1. How old was Abraham when Isaac was born?
   a. Fifty years old
   b. 100 years old
   c. 200 years old
   d. 400 years old

2. What did God make Sarah do?
   a. Cry   c. Laugh
   b. Scream   c. Sob

3. Why did Sarah ask Abraham to send Ishmael and Ishmael's mother, Hagar, out of the country?

4. Who told Abraham to listen to Sarah?

5. What did God do when Ishmael was crying because there was no water to drink?
   a. Told him not to cry
   b. Gave him water
   c. Sent down rain
   d. Promised to make him a great nation

6. When Ishmael's mother opened her eyes, what did she see?
   a. A river
   b. A well of water
   c. A waterfall
   d. A pond

7. What land did Ishmael's wife come out of?

8. When Ishmael grew up, what did he become?

9. What do the words "God is with you in everything that you do" mean?

10. What is a *ewe*?

11. Where was the well that Abraham dug?

12. How long did Abraham stay in the land of the Philistines?
    a. For 100 years
    b. For a few days
    c. For a long time
    d. He never stayed in the land of the Philistines

Why didn't Noah go fishing?

He only had two worms!

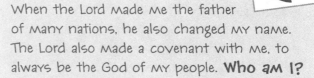

Who Am I?

When the Lord made me the father of many nations, he also changed my name. The Lord also made a covenant with me, to always be the God of my people. **Who am I?**

Abram (later Abraham)

Chapter 2 Answer Key

Travel by Ark
1. 450 feet long
2. a. Cypress
3. 75 feet wide
4. d. Pitch
5. Yes
6. Floodwaters
7. God made him a promise
8. b. Every kind
9. Noah's wife and his sons with their wives
10. One door
11. Food for his family and the animals
12. c. Three

Two by Two
1. At least two
2. True
3. Forty
4. Mount Ararat
5. c. In Turkey
6. A raven
7. d. A dove
8. An olive leaf
9. He built an altar
10. a. A goose
11. d. A horse
12. Over a year

A Rainbow
1. The people in Noah's family
2. Never to destroy the Earth with another flood
3. d. An agreement
4. The rainbow
5. Red, orange, yellow, green, blue, indigo, and purple
6. Black
7. Ham's grandson
8. a. Ham
9. Japheth
10. The Semites
11. d. In tents
12. c. He was a farmer

The Tower of Babel
1. a. One language
2. Shem's great-great-grandson
3. c. People began speaking different languages
4. b. A tower
5. d. Bricks
6. Tall enough to reach Heaven
7. Tar
8. By making them unable to understand each other's speech
9. He scattered them all over the Earth
10. Terah

Abram Follows
1. c. Sarai
2. a. No children
3. In Haran
4. a. Your relatives
5. To Abram's offspring
6. They went to Egypt
7. d. People don't have enough to eat
8. c. The pharaoh
9. d. Diseases
10. To Jordan
11. That the Lord would make Abram's family too large to count
12. One-tenth of everything

Do Not Be Afraid
1. He would protect Abram
2. b. He will manage it
3. Great, superior
4. c. Someone to inherit what he owns
5. Count the stars
6. He was worried because he had no children
7. b. A young cow
8. a. Iraq

Abram's Dream
1. c. A thick and dreadful darkness
2. d. Ishmael
3. Because Abraham would be a father of many nations
4. c. Sarah
5. c. To be their God
6. Isaac
7. Because they were evil and sinful
8. She turned into a pillar of salt
9. b. Speaks the Word of the Lord

Isaac Is Born
1. b. 100 years old
2. c. Laugh
3. To be sure that Isaac would inherit all of Abraham's property
4. God
5. d. Promised to make him a great nation
6. b. A well of water
7. Egypt
8. An archer
9. God will help you in all you do
10. A female sheep
11. In Beersheba
12. c. For a long time

A Time of Prayer

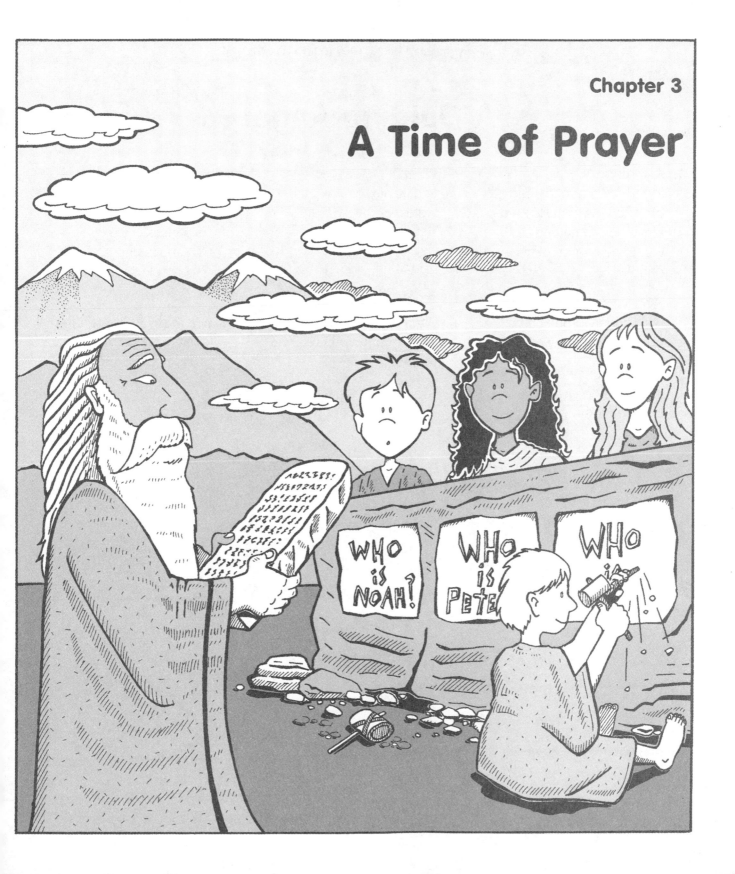

A Guiding Angel

1. If Abraham's servant found a woman for Isaac, but she was not willing to leave her homeland, would he be free of his oath?

2. What was outside of Nahor, where the women came out to draw their water?

3. To whom did the woman the Lord had chosen for Isaac offer the water?

4. What did the woman use to give him a drink of water?
   a. Her bowl
   b. Her palms
   c. Her jar
   d. Her goatskin

5. What did the servant give in exchange for their rooms?
   a. Gold   c. Brass
   b. Silver   d. Money

6. What was the jewelry Rebekah was given?
   a. A crown
   b. A necklace
   c. A nose ring and two bracelets
   d. A ring

7. Whom did Rebekah offer to feed and provide for?

camel count

How many camels loaded with presents did Abraham's faithful steward take to Mesopotamia to find a wife for Isaac? Using this picture as a guide, answer the math questions below to find out:

Count the number of CAMELS' FEET.

Divide by the number of HATS.

Multiply by the number of BEARDS.

Add the number of STRIPED ROBES.

Number of camels that went to Mesopotamia:

_____

A Prayer Is Answered

1. Why did Abraham's servant ask if they would deal kindly with his master's son?

2. Who decided whether Rebekah should marry?
   a. Her father
   b. Rebekah
   c. Abraham
   d. The Lord

3. When Rebekah's family asked her, what did she say?

4. How many people did her family say Rebekah would become the mother of?
   a. "Thousands upon thousands"
   b. "Hundreds of nations"
   c. "Dozens of people"
   d. "One or two people"

5. When Isaac saw Rebekah, what was he doing?
   a. Walking
   b. Working in the field
   c. Meditating
   d. Swimming in the river

6. Where did Isaac and Rebekah get married?
   a. In a cave
   b. In a house
   c. In a temple
   d. In a tent

7. How many sons did Abraham's son Ishmael have?

8. What did Isaac ask God for?

9. How did Rebekah's unborn children act?

10. What were the two nations the Lord told Rebekah of?

11. Which child did God say would serve the other?

Who Am I?

I was able to understand other people's dreams, but many people did not like this gift. It was not until I met the Pharaoh and told him of his dream that I was rewarded. **Who am I?**

Joseph

Fun Fact

Double Trouble

Being born a twin may be more common than you think. The odds are around one in ninety that you could have been a twin—and maybe you are. The Bible mentions several sets of twins throughout its many pages.

Isaac and Esau

1. What kind of twins did Rebekah and Isaac have?
   a. A boy and a girl
   b. Fraternal boy twins
   c. Identical boy twins
   d. They did not have twins

2. When Jacob was born, what part of Esau was he holding on to?
   a. His heel   c. His ear
   b. His hand   d. His toe

3. Why did Isaac like Esau?

4. What did Esau sell for food when he almost starved to death?

5. Why was a birthright so important?

6. What did the Philistines and Isaac's servants argue about?

7. Why did the king make a covenant with Isaac?

8. How did Rebekah and Isaac feel when Esau married a daughter of the Hittites?
   a. They were happy
   b. They were proud
   c. They were sad
   d. They didn't care

9. Why was it hard for Isaac to know who was in the room?
   a. He was deaf
   b. He was nearly blind
   c. He was sleeping
   d. It was dark

10. What did Rebekah cook for Isaac?

11. When Isaac asked Jacob how he found the goats so quickly, what was Jacob's response?

12. What did Isaac give Jacob when Jacob tricked him into thinking he was Esau?

TRY THIS ▶ Not a Mirror Image

Have you ever wondered what it would be like to be a twin? Did you know that even twins aren't exactly identical? And neither are the two halves of your body! Ask your parents for a picture of yourself that you can cut in half. Now, hold it up to a mirror. What do you see? Now, try measuring both of your legs or feet. Can you see any differences?

Tag the Twins

Like Esau and Jacob, twins don't have to look the same. But then again, some twins are identical in every way! See if you can find the two sets of twins on this playground. Here's what to look for:

- Two kids who look exactly the same, but are wearing different clothes.

- Two kids who look very different, but are wearing identical clothes.

Jacob's Dream

Words to Know

TRY THIS

1. After Jacob set out for Rebekah's homeland, he stopped to rest. What did he use for a pillow?
   a. A lambskin
   b. A piece of cloth
   c. A stone
   d. A shoe

2. While he was sleeping, what did Jacob dream of?

3. Who stood above the ladder?

4. What did God promise in the dream?

5. Which of the following did Jacob use to make a house for God?
   a. Bricks   c. Sand
   b. Tents   d. A pile of stones

6. Who did Jacob want to marry?

7. Who was Rachel's older sister?
   a. Leah   c. Rebekah
   b. Eve   d. Sarah

8. How many years was Jacob supposed to work for Laban before he could marry Rachel?
   a. Three   c. Seven
   b. Five   d. Ten

9. Who was the child born to Rachel?

10. Did Jacob want the spotted or the white animals?

11. Why was there a pillar between Laban and Jacob?

12. What did Laban want Jacob to remember?

▶ *Dream Interpretation*

Throughout history people have used dream interpretation to foretell the future or to explain a person's feelings. If you want to try your own dream interpretation you can jot down some of the things you remember from your recent dreams or those of your family or friends. Take the list to the library to look the items up in a dream interpretation book and find out what your dreams mean.

While Jacob prepares for a meeting with Esau, God wrestles with him and brings about a change. —Genesis 31:29–33:4

God's Camp

1. Why did Laban send so many animals with Jacob?

2. What does the word *Mahanaim* mean?

3. Where had Esau been living all this time?

4. How did Jacob feel when he heard Esau was coming to meet him with 400 men?

5. Did Jacob have a plan to protect his animals and family?

6. What did Jacob plan to do to Esau?
   a. Kill him
   b. Betray him
   c. Give him gifts
   d. Return his birthright

7. Which of the following would be the gifts for Esau?
   a. Pieces of gold
   b. Many animals
   c. Freedom
   d. Jewelry

8. What joint did the man who wrestled Jacob put out of place?
   a. His shoulder   c. His hip
   b. His finger   d. His knee

9. When the man blessed Jacob, what did Jacob say?

10. What did the man change Jacob's name to?
    a. Israel
    b. Jordan
    c. Daniel
    d. Herman

11. As Jacob lifted his eyes, he saw Esau run to hug him. What did they do next?

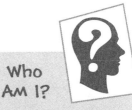

Who Am I?

I am a prophet with two names. One of the names belongs to a country now. I was a trickster, but with God's help changed for the better. I once had a dream about a ladder. **Who am I?**

(Jacob (later Israel))

TRY THIS

WHAT IS MY NAME?

▶ **Guess Who?**

Do you think you can tell people apart even if you can't see them? Try playing a game where you have to recognize your friends while blindfolded. Maybe you can guess by listening to their voices or maybe they will give you some clues. Then it's your turn to fool them.

Joseph, the son of Jacob, is betrayed by his brothers, and yet he forgives them. —Genesis 36:6–45:8

Asking Forgiveness

prophet: Someone who foretells the future. There are many prophets in the Bible who receive signs from God and share them with other people.

Words to Know

1. Why could Jacob and Esau no longer live in the same area?

2. Although Jacob had many children, one was his favorite. Do you know which one?
   a. Benjamin   c. Levi
   b. Dinah   d. Joseph

3. What did Jacob give Joseph to wear?
   a. A shield
   b. A coat of many colors
   c. A crown
   d. Jewels

4. One night Joseph had a dream. What did he see?

5. How did Joseph's brothers feel about his dream?

6. What did they do to punish Joseph?

7. When Jacob sent his sons to Egypt, who did they bow down to?

8. Why did Joseph set traps for his brothers?
   a. To gather food
   b. To test them
   c. To punish them
   d. For fun

Fun Fact

The Lord's Prayer

The Lord's Prayer appears twice in the Bible. It is said to be the most popular spoken prayer of all time and is well known throughout the world. Many believe it is also the most memorized prayer as well.

Joseph sends for his father to come to Egypt. While he is there, he names the twelve tribes of Israel. —Genesis 45:9–50:26

A Trip to Egypt

1. Why did Joseph tell his brothers to bring their father to Egypt?
   a. To prove he was alive
   b. To make his father proud
   c. To provide him with food
   d. To see him

2. Who told Joseph to bring his family to Egypt?

3. When did Joseph's father, Israel, start for Egypt?

4. How did God appear to Jacob?
   a. As an angel
   b. In a vision
   c. As a stranger
   d. In a fire

5. What was the country Jacob settled in?
   a. Goshen   c. Canaan
   b. Edom   d. Moab

6. Who did Joseph bring to Jacob for his blessing?

7. What did Joseph do when he went to see his very ill father?
   a. He looked at him
   b. He hugged him
   c. He kneeled to him
   d. He bowed to him

8. Which hand did Jacob use to bless Ephraim?

9. Why did Jacob bless Joseph's younger son?

10. After Jacob foretold the future for his sons and blessed them, what did he do next?

11. Although Joseph stayed in Egypt, where did he say God would place his brothers?

12. Who did Jacob ask to carry him out of Egypt, after his death?

Q. Where is the first tennis match mentioned in the Bible?

A. When Joseph served in Pharaoh's court.

Cottage Cheese

In the days of the Bible, cheese was discovered by accident. As the milk began to warm in the bottles, it would curdle, turning to cheese. To make your own cottage cheese, you need two cups of milk warmed in a pan on the stove. Add 1 teaspoon of rennet and stir. Remove the mixture from the heat and pour it into a dish to cool for thirty minutes. Using the top of a double boiler, reheat the mixture to a medium heat, forming curds. Remove from the heat and let cool. Pour the curds through a strainer lined with several layers of damp cheesecloth, then squeeze the curds in the cloth, removing any extra liquid. Pour the cheese in a bowl, and it's ready to eat.

A Baby in a Basket

ark: A ship or boat used for travel on water. Moses' basket was called an ark. The same name was also given to the boat that Noah made before the flood.

Words to Know

1. How many of the children of Israel had come into Egypt?
   a. Fifty people
   b. Seventy people
   c. 100 people
   d. 170 people

2. Why did the new pharaoh worry about the number of Israelites in Egypt?

3. How did the pharaoh try to keep them down?

4. Did the pharaoh's plan work?

5. When the pharaoh saw how many children were being born to the Israelites, what did he order?

6. One Israelite family had a baby boy, and they hid him from the Egyptians. How long were they able to hide him?

7. Then, his mother made a basket for the baby. What was it made of?
   a. Papyrus   c. Cloth
   b. Wood   d. Paper

8. Where did the mother place the basket with the baby in it?

9. Which family member waited to see what would happen to the baby?

10. Who saw the basket?
    a. An aunt
    b. Pharaoh's daughter
    c. Shiprah
    d. Puah

TRY THIS

▶ *Make Your Own Mini-Basket*

You can weave a mat or basket by using string licorice or fruit strips. First, lay several of these edible threads flat on a piece of cardboard, one beside the other in a line. You can tape down one end if you need to. Using extra threads, weave them over and under your other strips, from the other direction. Now you have a woven mat!

Baby in a Basket

Follow baby Moses from START to END to see that he gets safely down the river.

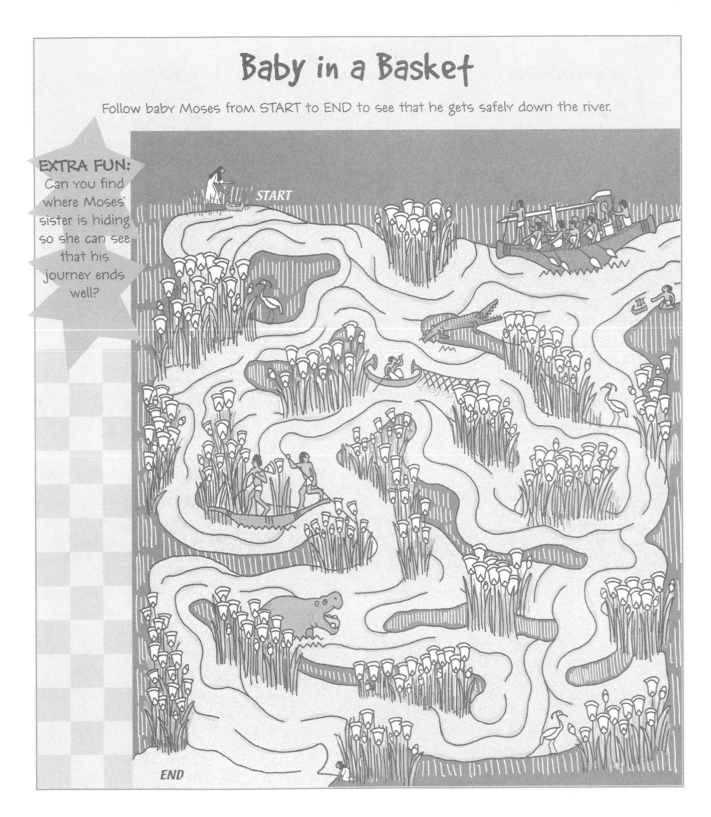

EXTRA FUN: Can you find where Moses' sister is hiding so she can see that his journey ends well?

START

END

Chapter 3 Answer Key

A Guiding Angel
1. Yes
2. A well
3. To Abraham's servant
4. c. Her jar
5. a. Gold
6. c. A nose ring and two bracelets
7. The animals

A Prayer Is Answered
1. So Rebekah could marry Isaac
2. d. The Lord
3. "I will go"
4. a. "Thousands upon thousands"
5. c. Meditating
6. d. In a tent
7. Twelve
8. A child
9. They struggled with each other
10. The two children she was carrying
11. The older would serve the younger

Isaac and Esau
1. b. Fraternal boy twins
2. a. His heel
3. Because he was a hunter and brought Isaac meat to eat
4. His birthright
5. It guarantees that the eldest son will inherit his father's property
6. Who owned the wells in the land
7. Because he feared him and he knew he was blessed by God
8. c. They were sad
9. b. He was nearly blind
10. Two young goats
11. "The Lord your God gave me success"
12. His blessing

Jacob's Dream
1. c. A stone
2. A ladder that went all the way up to Heaven with the angels of God going up and down
3. The Lord
4. To give that land to Jacob and to be with him wherever he went
5. d. A pile of stones
6. Rachel
7. a. Leah
8. c. Seven
9. Joseph
10. The spotted animals
11. It divided their land
12. That God was keeping a watch over them

God's Camp
1. He was frightened by a dream in which God came to visit him
2. "The camp of God"
3. In the country of Edom
4. He was afraid
5. Yes, he divided them into two groups and prayed for them
6. c. Give him gifts
7. b. Many animals
8. c. His hip
9. "I saw God face to face"
10. a. Israel
11. They wept

Asking Forgiveness
1. There was not enough land for all of their livestock
2. d. Joseph
3. b. A coat of many colors
4. His brothers' sheaves of grain were bowing down to his sheaf of grain
5. They were jealous and angry
6. They tore off his coat and sold him to a band of Ishmaelites
7. The governor, their brother Joseph
8. b. To test them

A Trip to Egypt
1. c. To provide him with food
2. The Pharaoh
3. As soon as he learned Joseph was alive
4. b. In a vision
5. a. Goshen
6. His two sons
7. d. He bowed to him
8. His right hand
9. He said he would become greater than his older brother
10. He named them the twelve tribes of Israel
11. In the land of Canaan
12. Joseph

A Baby in a Basket
1. b. Seventy people
2. He feared that during war the Israelites might join the enemy
3. He oppressed them and forced them to work very hard
4. No, the Israelites grew even stronger
5. That all baby boys should be thrown into the Nile
6. For three months
7. a. Papyrus
8. In the reeds on the riverbank
9. His sister
10. b. Pharaoh's daughter

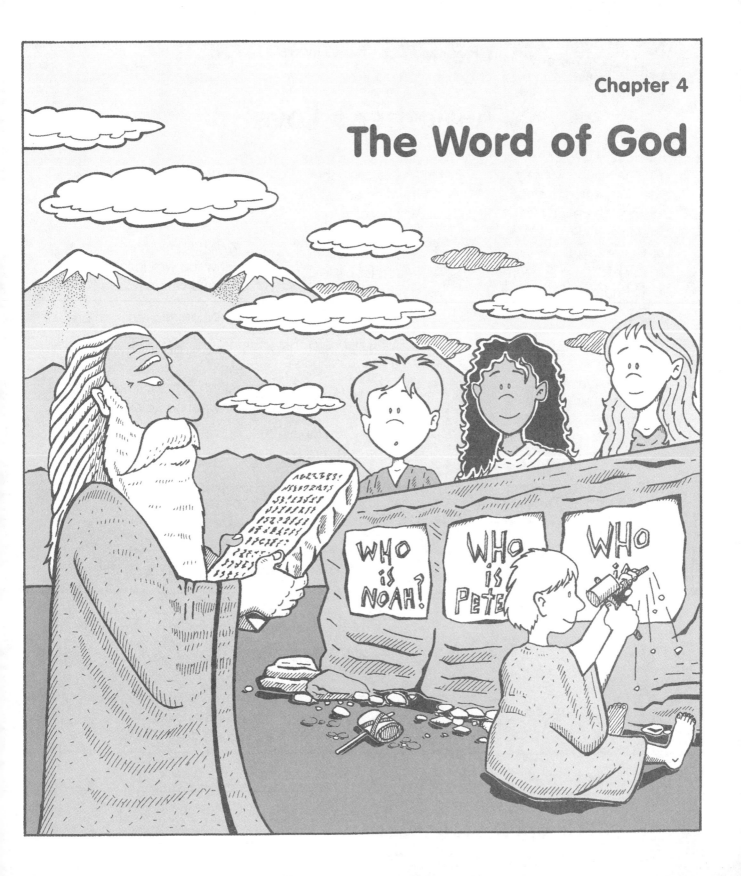

The Word of God

A Mother's Love

1. When the Hebrew baby was old enough to stop nursing, where did his sister take him?
   a. Out of Egypt
   b. Back to the river
   c. To Pharaoh's daughter to become her son
   d. To Canaan

2. As Moses grew older, what made him angry at the Egyptians?

3. Did Moses allow the torture to go on?
   a. Yes, because he agreed with it
   b. Yes, because he feared for his life
   c. No, he stopped it
   d. He did not care

4. Why did the Hebrews ask Moses if he was a judge?

5. How did the Hebrews feel about what Moses did?
   a. Sad   c. Happy
   b. Confused   d. Tired

6. What did Moses do when Pharaoh found out that he killed an Egyptian?

7. Whom did Moses meet by the well in the new land where he lived?

8. Whom did Moses marry?
   a. Dinah   c. Zipporah
   b. Leah   d. Ruth

9. When Moses had a son, what name did he give to him?

The Name Game

What was the meaning of the name that Pharoh's daughter gave to Moses? Use the decoder to figure out each letter and write the answer on the lines below.

God appeared to Moses in a flaming bush. He told him of
His plan to bring the people out of Egypt. —Exodus 3:1–4:3

A Bush on Fire

1. What did Moses take to the mountain of God?

2. When Moses saw the flames in a bush, how did he know something unusual was happening?

3. What did God say when He spoke to Moses from the flaming bush?

4. Who did the Lord say He was?

5. Why did Moses hide his face?
   a. He thought the flames were too hot
   b. He was afraid to look at God
   c. He was sorry for what he had done
   d. He was ashamed his face was dirty

6. What did God say He would do for His people?

7. Whom did God plan to send to Egypt in order to free the children of Israel?
   a. An angel
   b. Reuel
   c. Gershom
   d. Moses

8. If Moses would free the people, what did God promise they would have?

9. Whom did God want Moses and the elders to go and see?
   a. Aaron   c. Pharaoh
   a. Shiphrah d. Puah

10. How many people did Moses think would believe he saw the Lord?

11. When Moses threw the staff to the ground, what did it become?
    a. A river   c. A stone
    b. Gold   d. A serpent

TRY THIS ▶ A Secret Identity

Here's a fun name game to play with your friends at a party. First get a grownup to place a nametag with the name of a person from the Bible on each player's back. The fun begins when you give your friend a clue or two, or act something out, to help him guess which name is on his back. Then he can do the same for you. Once each player has guessed which name is on his back, ask the grownup to reveal the secret identities. The game isn't over until each person figures out his secret identity.

The Staff

Who Am I?

It was good that I was never afraid of heights, water, or fire. I have known two mothers and two fathers. I have felt the power and the love of God.
Who am I?

Moses

1. What happened when the Lord told Moses to grab the serpent by the tail?
   a. It turned to dust
   b. It disappeared
   c. It became a staff again
   d. It bit him

2. After God placed a skin disease on Moses' hand, what did Moses do?

3. When God told Moses to go and convince the people, what did Moses fear?

4. Who did God say should speak for Moses instead?
   a. God   c. An angel
   b. Reuel   d. Aaron

5. What did the Lord warn Moses about Pharaoh?

6. When the elders came, what made them believe Moses?

7. When Aaron and Moses spoke to Pharaoh, what did he do?

8. Who was blamed for Pharaoh's anger?

9. Did the people believe that God would free them?

10. What did the Pharaoh do when God had Moses turn his staff into a serpent?
    a. He fell to his knees
    b. He fainted
    c. He couldn't believe his eyes
    d. He refused to let the Hebrews go

11. When Moses touched his staff to the river Nile, what happened to the water?
    a. It turned to blood
    b. It became muddy
    c. It caused a flood
    d. Nothing happened

12. Was Moses the only person who could change the water?

Fun Fact

It's Raining Cats and Dogs

Did you know that there have been reports of frogs raining down from the sky? All kinds of other strange things have been said to rain down on us as well, including fish—and that's just one more good reason to carry an umbrella!

Frogs Everywhere

1. What did Pharaoh beg for when Egypt was covered in frogs?

2. When Pharaoh saw the frogs were gone, what did he do?
   a. He thanked the Lord
   b. He told Moses he believed in God
   c. He refused to listen to Moses and Aaron
   d. He had Moses arrested

3. What plague did the Lord send next?
   a. Gnats and flies
   b. Rain and thunder
   c. Mice and rats
   d. Worms and bugs

4. Were the magicians able to produce gnats or flies as the Lord had done?

5. After the gnats and flies, what plague came next?

6. When Pharaoh still would not free the people, what did the Lord send?

7. Which plague followed the boils?
   a. Floods   c. Fire
   b. Hail   d. Earthquakes

8. When the locusts came, what did they eat?

9. What did Pharaoh ask the brothers to beg the Lord to do?

10. How did Moses ask the Lord to remove the locusts?
   a. He prayed to Him
   b. He had Aaron talk to Him
   c. He threw his staff into the air
   d. He refused to ask the Lord to remove them

plague: An illness spread throughout a group of people, a terrible disaster, or problem. Many of the plagues mentioned in the Bible involve insects, animals, and nature.

Words to Know

Fun Fact

Light and Darkness

Since the ninth plague, the three days of darkness, it has never been dark for that long again. The only time we normally see darkness other than at night is during a solar eclipse. Solar eclipses only last a few minutes.

frogs Underfoot!

Ignore the numbers 1 through 9, and collect only the letters from left to right and top to bottom. Write each letter in order on the lines at the bottom of the page. When you're done, you'll have the answer to this riddle:

How would it feel to find everything covered with frogs?

_ _ _ _ _ _ _ _   _ _ _ _ _

Free at Last

1. In what direction did Moses stretch his hand so that there would be darkness?

2. After Pharaoh refused to allow Moses to have sacrifices, what did Moses say to Pharaoh?

3. How long did the darkness last?

4. How were the Hebrews instructed to mark their doorposts?

5. Whom did the Lord promise to save?

6. What were the people asked to eat for seven days?

7. Would anything happen to those who ate leavened bread during Passover?

8. After the plague of the firstborns, what did Pharaoh do?

9. What did the Egyptians want the Hebrews to take when they left?

10. How did the Lord show himself to the people?

11. When the children of Israel left Egypt, how many were there in all?

12. Why did Pharaoh follow the Hebrews to the bank of the Red Sea?

covenant: A promise or agreement between people or with God. God made many covenants or promises in the Bible. The rainbow was one of them.

Words to Know

Unleavened Bread

If you want to try making unleavened bread, you will need 1 cup of flour, ½ cup of water, a pinch of salt, and 1 teaspoon of margarine. Stir all the ingredients together in a bowl. Then, knead and roll your dough out into three flat circles. With the help of an adult, you can cook your flat breads brushed with a little margarine in a skillet on medium heat. When both sides of the bread are browned, remove the bread from the skillet, place it on a plate, and top it with honey or jam.

Sea of Red

1. How did Moses divide the sea?

2. As the Hebrews crossed the sea, what was to their left and right?

3. Which direction did the wind that dried the sea's bed come from?
   a. The south   c. The west
   b. The north   d. The east

4. When the Egyptians followed them into the middle of the sea, what did the Lord do?

5. Why did the Egyptians try to turn back?

6. What happened when the Hebrews reached the other side?

7. Who did the Hebrews believe had led them to safety?
   a. Moses c. The Pharaoh
   b. Aaron d. The Lord

8. Miriam used an instrument to lead the women in song and dance—what was it?
   a. A tambourine
   b. A drum
   c. Bells
   d. A guitar

9. When the people saw they had nothing to drink, to whom did they complain?
   a. To Moses
   b. To Abraham
   c. To God
   d. To the golden calf

10. How did the bitter water of this new wilderness become sweet?

11. Why did the Hebrews wish they were back in Egypt?

TRY THIS

▶ **Part the Red Sea**

If you want to make your own parting Red Sea, find a clean, clear twenty-ounce plastic soda bottle with a lid. Remove the label. While standing over a sink, pour 1 cup of oil and 1 cup of red colored water into the bottle. Then, screw the lid back on and make sure it's tight. Now, tip your bottle to see what happens. Store your Red Sea in a place where the oil can't spill.

The Lord provides food for the hungry children of Israel. —Exodus 16:4–17:5

Bread from the Sky

1. Moses and Aaron promised the Hebrews they would see something in the morning. What did they call it?

2. Moses felt that the people were complaining about something. What was it?

3. What did Moses ask Aaron to do?

4. When the Lord appeared to the Hebrews, what did they see?
   a. An angel   c. A cloud
   b. A fire   d. Thunderbolts

5. In the evening the Hebrews were given meat. What kind of meat was it?
   a. Quail   c. Pork
   b. Goat   d. Beef

6. When the dew left in the morning, what was in its place?

7. What was the food that fell from the sky called?

8. Were the Hebrews allowed to keep any extra bread?
   a. Yes
   b. No
   c. Only if Moses let them
   d. Only if they were hungry

9. Why did the Lord provide extra food on the sixth day?

10. How long did the Hebrews eat the manna?
   a. Twenty days
   b. Forty days
   c. Forty years
   d. Until this day

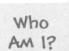

Who Am I?

I am a brother to Moses, and the one who helped him free the children of Israel from Egypt. I also helped him hold his hands in the sky during a battle for Israel and spoke the words of God for him. **Who am I?**

Aaron

What kind of fruit did Noah bring on the ark?

Pears (pairs)!

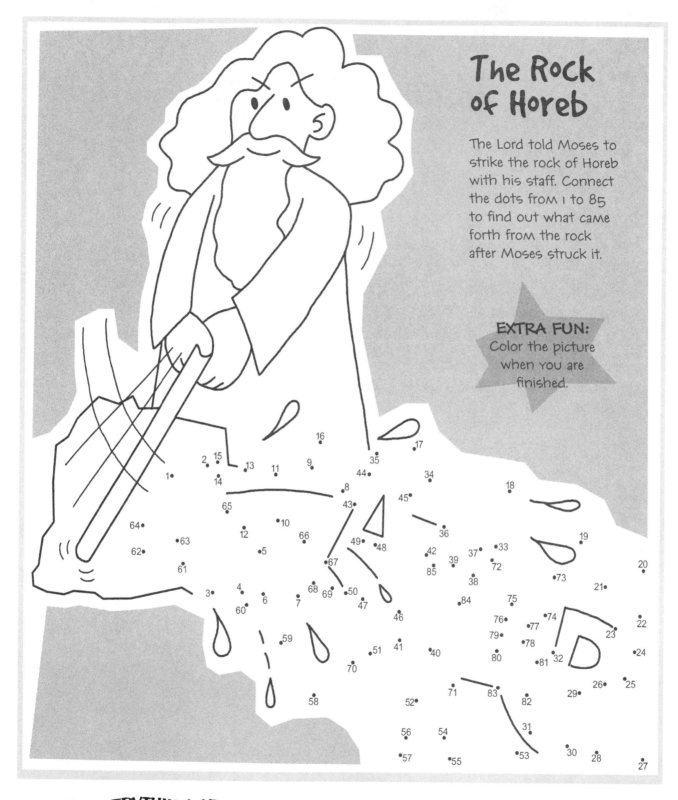

The Rock of Horeb

The Lord told Moses to strike the rock of Horeb with his staff. Connect the dots from 1 to 85 to find out what came forth from the rock after Moses struck it.

EXTRA FUN: Color the picture when you are finished.

On the Mountain

1. What was the name of the place where the Hebrews camped near the mountain?

2. When God called down to Moses, where did the voice come from?

3. What message did God have for him?

4. On what birds' wings did God say He brought the people of Israel to Him?
   a. Eagles   c. Ducks
   b. Doves   d. Hawks

5. Would Israel receive anything in return for following God?

6. Did the people agree to follow God's wishes?

7. Why did the Lord say He would come to the people as a thick cloud?

8. How many days did the people have to get ready for God's arrival?
   a. Two   c. Seven
   b. Three   d. Ten

9. What did the Lord warn Moses not to do?

10. How did they know it was time for the Lord's visit?
    a. There was lightning and thunder
    b. A trumpet blared
    c. The world was silent
    d. Both a and b

decree: An order or decision given by a judge. There were many people who were judges in the Bible. Moses was one of the more famous ones.

Words to Know

TRY THIS ▶ **A Volcano of Your Own**

To make an exploding mountain or volcano, tape the bottom of a Styrofoam cup to a piece of cardboard. After, form some modeling clay around the cup to make a volcano shape. It's best to make your volcano erupt outside. To set up the eruption, add 4 teaspoons of baking soda with a drop of red food coloring. When you're ready for it to overflow, add ½ cup vinegar and watch what happens next!

Chapter 4 Answer Key

A Mother's Love

1. c. To Pharaoh's daughter to become her son
2. Their cruelty to the Hebrews
3. c. No, he stopped it
4. He stopped a fight between them
5. b. Confused
6. He fled the country so Pharaoh couldn't kill him
7. The daughters of the priest of Midian
8. c. Zipporah
9. Gershom

A Bush on Fire

1. A flock of sheep
2. The bush was on fire but did not burn
3. That Moses was standing on holy ground
4. The God of Abraham, Isaac, and Jacob
5. b. He was afraid to look at God
6. He would deliver them from Egypt
7. d. Moses
8. "A land flowing with milk and honey"
9. c. Pharaoh
10. None
11. d. A serpent

The Staff

1. c. It became a staff again
2. He cured it himself
3. That no one would listen to him
4. d. Aaron
5. That Pharoah's heart would harden
6. Aaron showed them the signs of God
7. He made the Hebrews work harder
8. Moses and Aaron
9. No
10. d. He refused to let the Hebrews go
11. a. It turned to blood
12. No, Egyptian magicians did the same thing

Frogs Everywhere

1. For Moses to pray for God to take the frogs away
2. c. He refused to listen to Moses and Aaron
3. a. Gnats and flies
4. No
5. The livestock plague
6. Boils
7. b. Hail
8. Every herb, fruit, and all of green from the trees
9. To remove the locusts
10. a. He prayed to Him

Free at Last

1. Toward the sky
2. "I will never appear before you again"
3. Three days
4. With the blood of a lamb
5. The Hebrews
6. Unleavened bread
7. They would be cut off from Israel
8. He let the people go
9. Anything that they needed
10. As a cloud by day and a fire by night
11. 600,000
12. He changed his mind and wanted them back as slaves

Sea of Red

1. He stretched his hand out over the water
2. Walls of water
3. d. The east
4. He slowed them down
5. They knew the Lord was helping the Hebrews
6. The water rushed back into place
7. d. The Lord
8. a. A tambourine
9. a. To Moses
10. God showed Moses a piece of wood to throw into the water
11. They wanted food to eat

Bread from the Sky

1. The glory of the Lord
2. God
3. Gather the Hebrews together to talk to them
4. c. A cloud
5. a. Quail
6. Round dry flakes of bread
7. Manna
8. b. No
9. So the Hebrews could stay inside on the Sabbath (seventh day)
10. c. Forty years

On the Mountain

1. The Desert of Sinai
2. The mountain
3. To tell the children of Israel that they should obey God and keep His covenant
4. a. Eagles
5. They would be special to God and become a holy nation
6. Yes
7. So the people could hear their God
8. b. Three days
9. Let the people go up the mountain
10. d. Both a and b

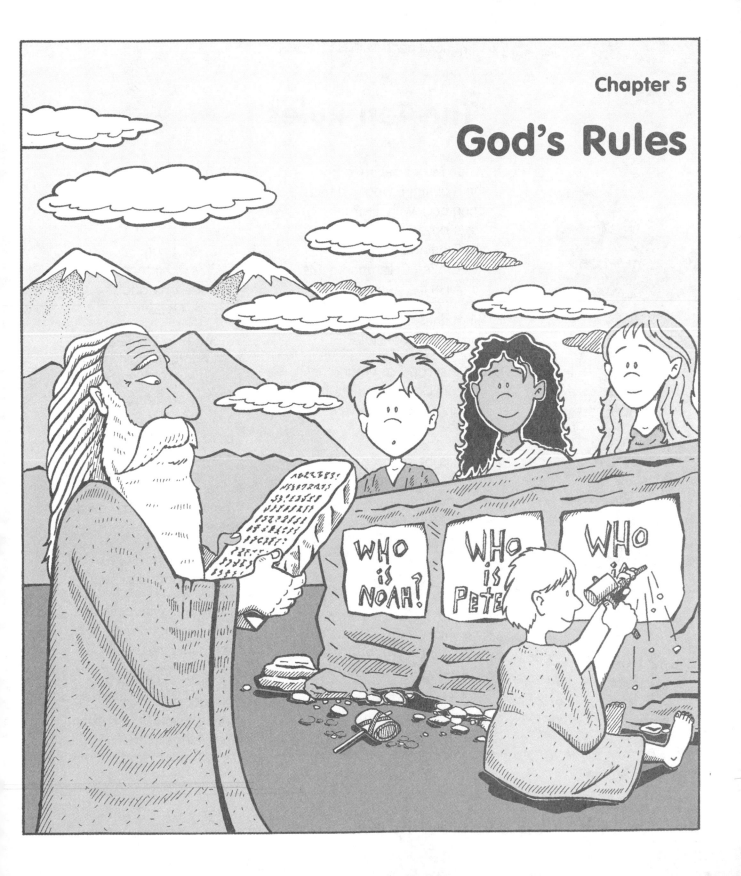

The Ten Rules

1. When Moses returned from the mountain, what did he bring back with him?
   a. A dove
   b. Food and water
   c. The Ten Commandments
   d. All of the above

2. What does the first commandment state?

3. In the second commandment, why did God declare that the people could not serve other gods?

4. What is the message of the third commandment?

5. In the fourth commandment God tells His people to "remember the Sabbath" and do what?
   a. Keep it holy
   b. Save their money
   c. Raise only goats
   d. Love God

6. Whom does the fifth commandment ask you to honor?
   a. Your brother as yourself
   b. Your father and mother
   c. Your elders
   d. Your countrymen

7. In the sixth commandment, what does God say you shall not do?

8. What is the message of the seventh commandment?

9. According to the ninth and tenth commandments, who should you treat well?

10. In addition to the Ten Commandments, were there more rules from God about other things?

Who Am I?

It has been said that my heart is not soft. Even plagues did not seem to faze me, not until the darkness came. By then it was too late to change. **Who am I?**

Pharaoh

The Tallest Mountain

Do you know what the tallest mountain in the world is? If you guessed Mount Everest, you're right. Mount Everest reaches a height of 29,000 feet. Mount Sinai, at about 7,500 feet, is much smaller.

God sends an Angel to guide the people to a special place that has been prepared for them. —Exodus 23:20–25:9

God's Angel

1. Whom did the Lord send to help the people obey His laws?
   - a. A judge
   - b. An angel
   - c. One more child of Moses
   - d. A special messenger

2. If the people listened to the angel, from whom would they be protected?

3. The Angel was sent for more than one reason. What was the second reason?

4. When they came to the new place, other people were already there. Did the Lord want the other people to stay or to go?

5. Where did Moses keep the words of God?
   - a. In the Book of the Covenant
   - b. In his mind
   - c. In his heart
   - d. In his suitcase

6. In the morning, Moses built an altar out of twelve pillars. Why did he use twelve pillars?

7. When Moses returned to the mountain, he took several others with him. Who were they?

8. How long did the cloud cover Mount Sinai before the Lord called Moses up again?
   - a. One year
   - b. One month
   - c. One week
   - d. One day

9. How much time did Moses spend on top of the mountain?
   - a. Forty days and forty nights
   - b. One year
   - c. Forty hours
   - d. Forty years

10. What gifts did the Lord ask of His people as an offering?

11. How did God want the people to build the dwelling of the Lord?

cherubim: Small, childlike angels with wings. There are cherubim that guard the gates of Eden and the Ark of the Covenant. They could also be seen in several places throughout the tabernacles.

Words to Know

Guiding Angel

The Lord has prepared a special place for His people, and sent an angel to guide them.
The angel who knows the way has all of the following features:

- a long robe
- an oval halo
- seven feathers in her wing
- a pattern of stars on her robe
- shoes

God tells the people how to build the ark and the tabernacle of the Lord. —Exodus 25:10–32:3

The Ark of the Covenant

1. When the Lord asked the children of Israel to make an ark, where was it going to be kept?

2. The ark was made of wood, but it was covered by metal. Which type of metal was it?
   a. Silver   c. Bronze
   b. Gold   d. Copper

3. What was to be placed inside the ark after it was built?

4. Soon, where would Moses find God dwelling?
   a. On the mountain
   b. In their hearts
   c. Between the cherubim above the ark
   d. Within eighty feet of the ark

5. What did the tabernacle look like?

6. In what way were the boards used for the sanctuary different?

7. What did the Lord instruct Moses to use to make the rooms and the door of the tabernacle?

8. Where did God tell Moses to place the ark?

9. What did God want in the second room of the tabernacle?

10. How were the tablets of the commandments written?
    a. "By the finger of God"
    b. "Stamped by Moses"
    c. "Carved by Aaron"
    d. "Chiseled by ten Israelite artists"

11. Why did the children of Israel grow restless?

12. What did the people ask Aaron to make?
    a. Food from the sky
    b. A deep well
    c. Some gods to go before them
    d. A temple

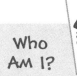

Who Am I?

I am the mother of twins who were double trouble. My grandson could understand others' dreams and soon became governor of Egypt. **Who am I?**

Rebekah

Fun Fact

An Unsolved Mystery

At this time, the location of the Ark of the Covenant remains unknown. After all, who would expect someone to hand over a gold-covered treasure such as this? Whatever the fate of the Ark, it's possible that one day we will all be able to see it for ourselves.

False Idols

Words to Know

Who Am I?

When I asked the Lord to help me be a good judge, I was blessed with knowledge and with wealth. Like my father David, I became a king. **Who am I?**

Solomon

1. Where did Aaron get the gold to make the golden calf?

2. What did Aaron build for the calf?
   a. A sanctuary
   b. A golden barn
   c. An altar
   d. A tent

3. Why was Moses upset when he returned from the mountain?

4. How did the Lord feel about what the people had done?

5. What did Moses ask God to do?
   a. To forgive the people
   b. To forget what had happened
   c. To remove the false idol
   d. To punish the people

6. When Moses saw the calf, he threw the tablets to the ground. What happened to them?

7. What did Moses do to the golden calf?
   a. He hid it
   b. He sold it
   c. He destroyed it
   d. He carried it up the mountain

8. When Moses asked the people to choose which side they were on, did everyone pick the Lord's side?

9. How did the people know when God was in the tabernacle?

10. What did the Lord ask Moses?

The Golden Rule

1. What were the Ten Commandments supposed to teach God's people?

2. Where in the fields were the people told they should not reap the crops?
   a. Every other row
   b. By the edges
   c. In the corners
   d. In the middle

3. Why did God tell the Israelites they should leave some grapes on the vines?

4. Did the Lord believe that cheating was the same as a lie?
   a. Yes
   b. No
   c. It depends

5. When were the wages of a hired man to be paid?

6. According to God, to whom are we supposed to be kind?
   a. To our enemies
   b. To the blind and deaf
   c. To those who betray us
   d. To our pets

7. How were the Hebrews asked to treat the poor and the rich?

8. Were the people allowed to tell tales against other Hebrews?

9. If one Hebrew hated another, was this all right with God, as long as it was kept secret?

10. What did God say about carrying a grudge?

TRY THIS

Miracle Fire

Fun Fact

Fire, smoke, and clouds were everywhere in the Bible. God created these fires and clouds as proof of His miracles. The only way humans can create fire is with a tool, such as a match or flint.

▶Who's Telling the Truth?

Have your friends or family play the game known as *Who's Telling the Truth and Who's Lying?* To play all you need are three contestants and a person who is guessing. The contestants need to tell one little-known fact about themselves or something they have just made up. Then the guesser must decide which of the three are lying and which are telling the truth. The winner is the contestant who fools the guesser most often.

Great Rewards

1. Did God's rules tell the people how to live their daily lives?
   a. Not exactly
   b. Yes
   c. No
   d. The answer is unknown

2. How could God help the Hebrews with their crops?

3. Would the people have enough food to last from season to season?

4. How much food did God promise?

5. God also promised to drive something else away. Do you know what that was?

6. When God spoke about their fear, how much fear would they have?
   a. They would always have some
   b. They would have no fear
   c. Their fear would be less
   d. They would be more afraid than ever

7. What would God offer as a reward?
   a. Money
   b. A new knowledge
   c. The return to the Garden of Eden
   d. His favor

8. When the Lord asked the Hebrews to remember something about Egypt, what was it?

Gifts from the Trees

Mrs. Fruitos is dressed in her Sunday best. Can you find the seven kinds of fruit that make Mrs. Fruitos look so sweet? Unscrambling the fruit names below will give you a hand.

NANBAA   CEPAH
_____   _____

EPAPL   UPLM
_____   _____

GNORAE   YRECHR
_____   _____

REPA
_____

HINT: Look carefully—some of the fruit is in slices!

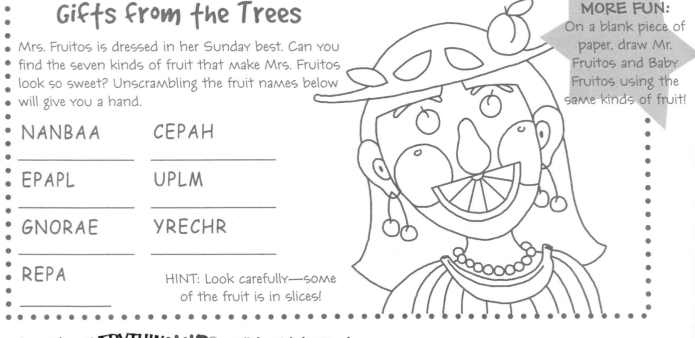

MORE FUN: On a blank piece of paper, draw Mr. Fruitos and Baby Fruitos using the same kinds of fruit!

A woman finds a way to help the Hebrews by telling others the truth of her people's fear. —Joshua 1:1–2:24

Telling the Truth

1. What did God want Joshua to do after the death of Moses?

2. Between whom did God want Joshua to divide the promised land?
   a. Everyone in the world
   b. Joshua and Aaron
   c. All the children of Israel
   d. Nobody

3. According to Joshua, who had commanded that the land be shared?

4. To where did Joshua send two men as spies?
   a. Egypt   c. Canaan
   b. Jericho   d. Jordan

5. Who hid the spies from the king?

6. How did the king of Jericho find out where the spies were staying?
   a. He saw them
   b. The house caught fire
   c. They didn't hide well enough
   d. Someone told him

7. Where in her house did the woman hide the men?
   a. Beneath her roof
   b. In the basement
   c. In the closet
   d. Under the bed

8. Why did the woman let the spies in?

9. When the woman told them the truth, what happened to the people of Jericho?

10. How did the spies repay the woman for her kindness?

11. What did they use to make their escape from Jericho?

12. When the spies returned to Joshua, what did they say?

Milk and Honey Shakes

In the Bible they speak of Canaan as the land of milk and honey. With all that milk and honey, they may have made milk and honey shakes. You can make one too. Get a blender and fill it with ½ cup of ice, ½ cup of milk, 1 teaspoon of honey, and ½ cup of strawberries or orange juice concentrate. Then blend and drink.

On the Jordan River

1. What did the Lord want to show Joshua?

2. What did the Lord want all of Israel to know about Himself?

3. What did Joshua tell the Hebrews?

4. Who was supposed to bear the Ark of the Covenant until the Hebrews were standing in the middle of the Jordan River?
   a. The priests
   b. Joshua and Aaron
   c. The women of Israel
   d. The men of Israel

5. How were the priests able to stand on dry ground?

6. Who was allowed to pass over the Jordan?
   a. No one
   b. All of the Israelites
   c. Only the kids
   d. Only the priests

7. How many men from each of the tribes of Israel did the Lord want Joshua to choose?
   a. Twenty   c. Seven
   b. Twelve   d. Three

8. What were the chosen men asked to do?

9. Why did Joshua place twelve stones in the middle of the river?

10. Did the Hebrews now fear Joshua, as they had feared Moses?
    a. No
    b. Only some of them
    c. Yes
    d. It's hard to say

11. During the forty years in the wilderness, did any of the warriors from Egypt come to Canaan?

12. When was the last time the children of Israel ate manna?

TRY THIS ▶ *The Domino Effect*

Have you ever heard of the domino effect? It means that one thing leads to another, which leads to another, and so on—such as, if you line up a bunch of dominos and push the first one, all of the subsequent dominos will fall down. If you want to create a domino effect on your own but don't have a domino set, wafer cookies will work just as well. Stand your rectangular-shaped cookies up on end, very close to each other, making a wall or line. When the time is right, push the first one to make it fall, and all the rest will follow.

Stones from the River

The Lord told Joshua to take twelve stones from the river Jordan. These stones would remind the people that the river was rolled back so that the ark of the covenant could be carried on dry ground. Use the clues to figure out which twelve stones were chosen.

- Cross off each letter that appears two times.
- Cross off each vowel.

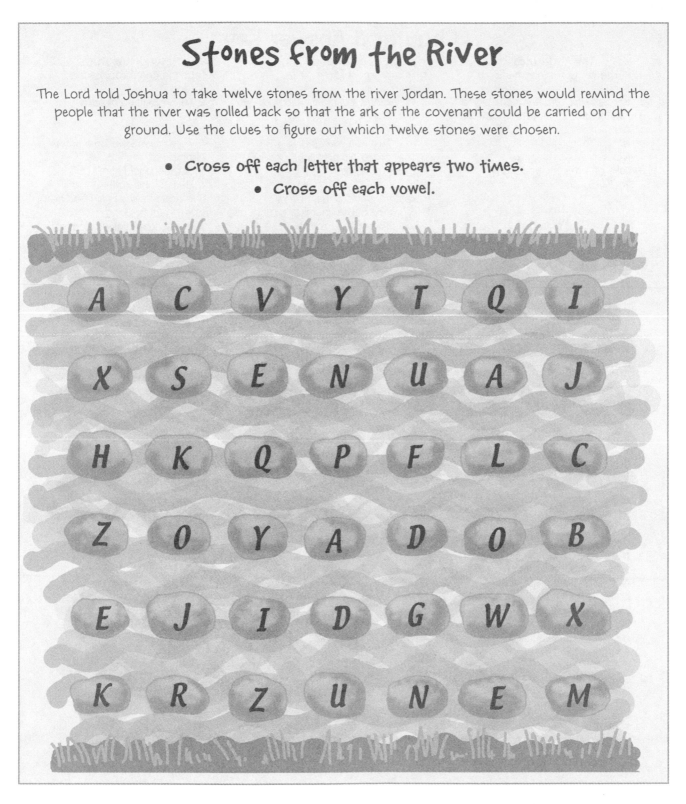

A	C	V	Y	T	Q	I
X	S	E	N	U	A	J
H	K	Q	P	F	L	C
Z	O	Y	A	D	O	B
E	J	I	D	G	W	X
K	R	Z	U	N	E	M

Chapter 5 Answer Key

The Ten Rules
1. c. The Ten Commandments
2. There is only one God
3. Because the Lord is a jealous God
4. Not to curse in the Lord's name
5. a. Keep it holy
6. b. Your father and mother
7. Murder
8. Love only the one you marry
9. Your neighbor
10. Yes

God's Angel
1. b. An angel
2. From their enemies
3. To guide the Hebrews to a prepared place
4. He wanted them to go, slowly
5. a. In the Book of the Covenant
6. One for each of the tribes of Israel
7. Aaron, Nadab, Abihu, and seventy elders
8. c. One week
9. a. Forty days and forty nights
10. Metals, jewels, and fine cloth
11. By the pattern God gave to them

The Ark of the Covenant
1. In the sanctuary they were to build
2. b. Gold
3. The tablets inscribed with the Ten Commandments of the Lord
4. c. Between the cherubim above the ark
5. It was a tent made of curtains and covered with goatskins
6. They were covered in gold and set in bases lined with silver
7. A gold-covered pillar with veils hanging from them
8. In the most holy place in the tabernacle
9. A golden candlestick, a table, and an altar
10. a. "By the finger of God"
11. Because Moses had been gone for so long
12. c. Some gods to go before them

False Idols
1. From the people
2. c. An altar
3. He learned that the people had worshipped the calf
4. Betrayed and angry
5. a. To forgive the people
6. They broke into pieces
7. c. He destroyed it
8. No
9. A cloud would appear over it
10. To tell the people that they must worship no other gods

The Golden Rule
1. To respect God and each other
2. b. By the edges
3. For strangers or the poor
4. a. Yes
5. As soon as the work was done
6. b. To the blind and deaf
7. The same way
8. No
9. No
10. He warned against it

Great Rewards
1. b. Yes
2. By bringing rain at the right times
3. Yes
4. All that they could eat
5. The savage beasts
6. b. They would have no fear
7. d. His favor
8. That it was God that made them free

Telling the Truth
1. Lead the people across the Jordan River
2. c. All the children of Israel
3. Moses
4. b. Jericho
5. A woman who lived in a house near the city wall
6. d. Someone told him
7. a. Beneath her roof
8. She said that she knew God had given them this land
9. They became faint with fear of the Hebrews and their God
10. They placed a scarlet cord at her window, as a mark to spare her
11. A window
12. That the people were full of fear because they knew God had given the land to the Hebrews

On the Jordan River
1. How valuable he was to God
2. That He is the God of Moses and the God of Joshua
3. That the living God was among them
4. a. The priests
5. The River Jordan's water was cut off from above and below
6. b. All of the Israelites
7. b. Twelve
8. To take stones out of the bed of the Jordan River as a memorial
9. To mark where the priests had stood
10. c. Yes
11. No
12. Before the Passover of the plains of Jericho

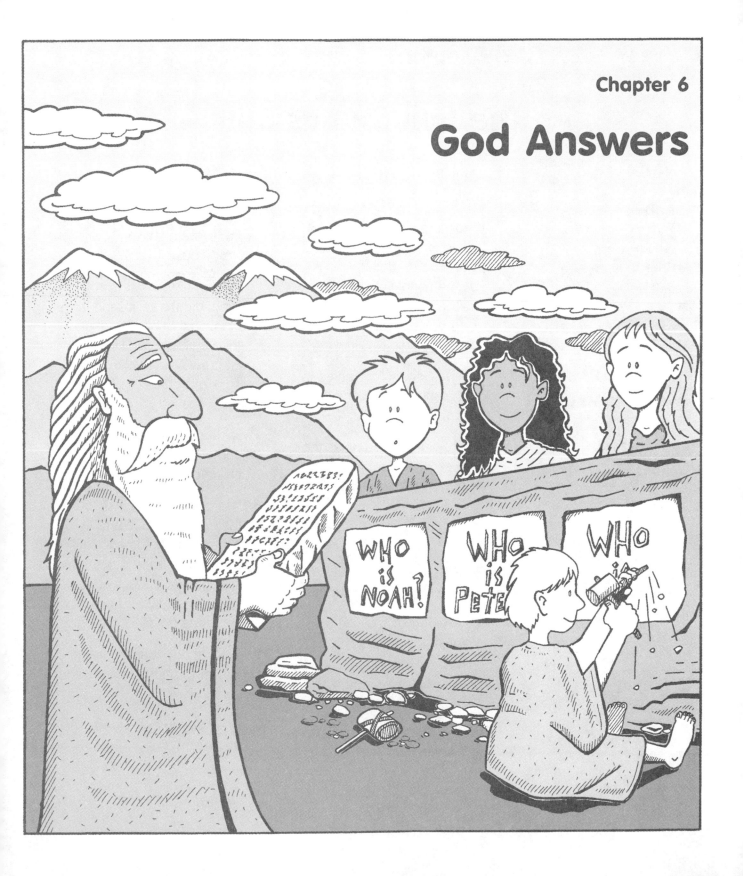

The Sun Stands Still

holy: To be holy is to be of a divine or sacred nature. The Bible speaks of the Holy Place, the Holy Ghost, and the Holy Spirit. All that is holy in the Bible is good and of God.

Words to Know

1. What did Joshua do after the walls of Jericho fell?

2. Who were the people that tricked the Hebrews into a treaty and an oath?
   a. The people of Ai
   b. The people of Hebron
   c. The people of Gibeon
   d. The people of Gilgal

3. The five kings who wanted to fight Joshua at Gibeon were from which tribe?

4. Where was Joshua when the men of Gibeon sent word for help to fight the five kings?

5. When did Joshua's army arrive?
   a. At dawn
   b. In the night
   c. At dusk
   d. At noontime

6. What did the Lord send from Heaven that hurt more people than the swords of the Hebrews?
   a. Hailstones   c. Lightning
   b. Frogs   d. Winds

7. Joshua asked the Lord to do something in the sight of the children of Israel—what was it?

8. The people of Israel defeated their enemies because the sun did not go down. How many days passed before it set again?
   a. Four days   c. Two days
   b. Three days   d. One day

9. On that day, the Lord listened to a man and fought for what country?

10. Has the sun ever stood still again?

Hail, Hail!

When hail comes down from the sky, it can be quite small, like the size of peas, or very large—as large as melons! The most common kind of hail is about the size of golf balls. These hailstones or balls of ice weigh in at several pounds and can be very dangerous to someone caught out in a storm.

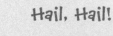

Fun Fact

The Weak Become Strong

1. Why did God let the Midianites rule over the Hebrews?

2. What did the Midianites do to make the Hebrews cry out to the Lord?
   a. They kicked them out
   b. They took their food
   c. They burned their homes
   d. They cursed the Lord

3. Whom did God send to the Hebrews to remind them of all the things He had done for them?
   a. A prophet   c. A king
   b. A soldier   d. An angel

4. When Gideon was in Ophrah, who appeared to tell him that God was answering their cry?

5. What did Gideon say God had done to the Hebrews?

6. Why did Gideon ask God for a sign?

7. What was the sign that the Lord sent to Gideon?

8. Why did Gideon destroy the altar that his father had built?

9. How many people did Gideon gather together to fight the Midianites?
   a. 3,200   c. 3.2 million
   b. 32,000   d. 32 million

10. God feared that the Hebrews would say what?

11. How many men did God tell Gideon to bring to the battle?
    a. Everyone he could find
    b. 10,000 men
    c. 300 men
    d. Three men

12. When the Lord turned the Midianites and their swords against each other, what happened?

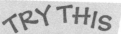

▶ **Dried Snacks**

Throughout history people have made dried foods to store them for long periods of time. Raisins are dried grapes and prunes are dried plums. You can dry your own foods with an oven. With the help of a grownup, place fruit slices on a cookie sheet in the oven turned on "warm" for a few hours. You can use apples, grapes, or chunk pineapple, or you can purée pears or strawberries in a blender. Once you have dried your fruit, you can store it in a resealable bag until you need a snack.

The Strength of Samson

1. Why were the children of Israel ruled by the Philistines?

2. Did the angel of the Lord who appeared before Samson's mother tell her who he was?

3. When the angel told Samson's mother that she would have a son, what did he say she should never do?
   a. Leave him alone
   b. Feed him unleavened bread
   c. Let anyone cut his hair
   d. Speak to strangers

4. From which group of people was Samson's wife?

5. What kind of problem did Samson ask the Philistines to solve?
   a. A riddle
   b. A jigsaw puzzle
   c. A maze
   d. A trivia question

6. How did the Philistines find out the answer to the problem?

7. To save his life, what did Samson reach for?

   a. A sword
   b. The jawbone of a donkey
   c. An arrow
   d. A spear

8. How did the Philistines learn the secret of Samson's strength?

9. What caused Samson to lose his strength?

10. Why did the Philistines bring him to their temple?

11. How did Samson destroy their temple?

Strong Samson, Weak Samson

Poor Samson! He loses his strength when his hair is cut. See if you can find the path from START to END, alternating strong Samson with weak Samson. You can go side to side or up and down, but not diagonally. Stop and try another path if you come to a pair of scissors.

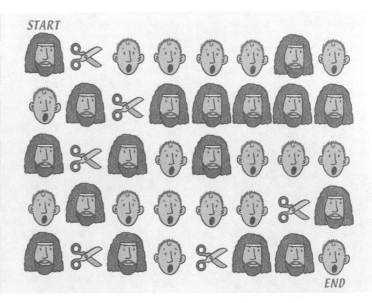

Ruth's Promise

1. What caused Naomi and her family to leave Israel and move to Moab?
   a. A plague
   b. A famine
   c. A flood
   d. An accident

2. Years later, why did Naomi decide to leave Moab?

3. What did Naomi hear that the Lord was giving to people of Israel?
   a. Jewels
   b. New homes
   c. Food
   d. New clothes

4. When she planned to leave for Israel, what did Naomi want her daughters-in-law to do?

5. Did both of the women choose to go with Naomi?
   a. Yes   b. No
   c. At first they both chose to go, but one changed her mind
   d. At first they both chose not to go, but then one changed her mind

6. What did Ruth tell her mother-in-law?

7. Ruth told Naomi something else too. What was it?

8. When they returned to Bethlehem, how did Ruth help out?
   a. By tending sheep
   b. By gleaning fields
   c. By weaving cloth
   d. By cleaning houses

9. What was the name of the owner of the field?
   a. Mahlon
   b. Elimelech
   c. Jeremiah
   d. Boaz

10. Why did the field's owner think Ruth was special?

11. What did the owner of the land ask Ruth to do?

12. What was the name of Boaz and Ruth's great-grandson?

Q. Who was the greatest comedian in the Bible?

A. Samson. He brought the house down.

Putting an End to Hunger

Famines have existed for thousands of years. Some famines are short, while others seem endless. Many organizations are working on ways to stop world hunger by sharing all of the food and water on Earth. They hope to someday rid the world of famines.

Fun Fact

A King of Hearts

God: In the Bible, God is the creator of man and the Earth. Some Christians believe in the Holy Trinity of God the Father, God the Son, and God the Holy Spirit. Most religions worship an eternal God or ruler of the universe.

Words to Know

1. What caused the Lord to feel sorry?

2. Why did God send the prophet, Samuel, to Bethlehem?

3. What did God tell Samuel to give as a sacrifice?
   a. A heifer   c. A goat
   b. A lamb   d. A pig

4. Who told Samuel to invite Jesse and his sons to the sacrifice?

5. What did the Lord say about how He chose a king?

6. Which part of a man did God think was important?

7. Where was Jesse's youngest son when Samuel told them to bring him to the sacrifice?
   a. Playing the harp
   b. Tending the sheep
   c. Repairing a tent
   d. Sleeping

8. What words did the Lord say to Samuel when he saw David?

9. When David was chosen by God, what left Saul and entered David?

10. When the good spirit left Saul and an evil spirit came, how did Saul feel?
    a. Ill   c. Happy
    b. Excited   d. Tired

11. What instrument did David play to make the evil spirit leave Saul?
    a. A tambourine
    b. A harp
    c. A trumpet
    d. Drums

The Giant

1. When the Philistines and the Hebrews gathered for battle, where were they?
   a. In the land of Gilead
   b. In the land of the Amorites
   c. In the hills of Israel
   d. By the Red Sea

2. What was the name of the Philistines' giant warrior?
   a. Abner   c. Joab
   b. Goliath   d. David

3. How tall was the giant?

4. What did the man that walked in front of the giant carry?

5. How many days did he challenge the Israelites?
   a. Two   c. Thirty
   b. Twelve   d. Forty

6. What did the giant say would happen to the losers of the battle?

7. How did King Saul and the Israelites feel about those words?

8. As David's older brothers left for the battle, where did David go?

9. Why did David go to the battlefield?

10. What did Goliath do to make David want to fight him?

11. How did David convince Saul that he should fight Goliath?

12. When Goliath was struck down, what did the Philistines do?
    a. They kept fighting
    b. They bowed to David
    c. They ran away
    d. They disappeared

TRY THIS

▶ *A Giant of a Party*

How about having a "giant" party? Everything in your party would be gigantic—a giant pizza, a contest for the best decorated giant cookie, a giant game of seeing how many people you can fit into a giant box, and a giant game of giant volleyball with a giant balloon. You can also have a "who can find the biggest thing" contest too—the biggest shoe, biggest leaf, biggest rock, and so on. Then, top it all off with a super-big giant sundae made and shared by all.

The Big Battle

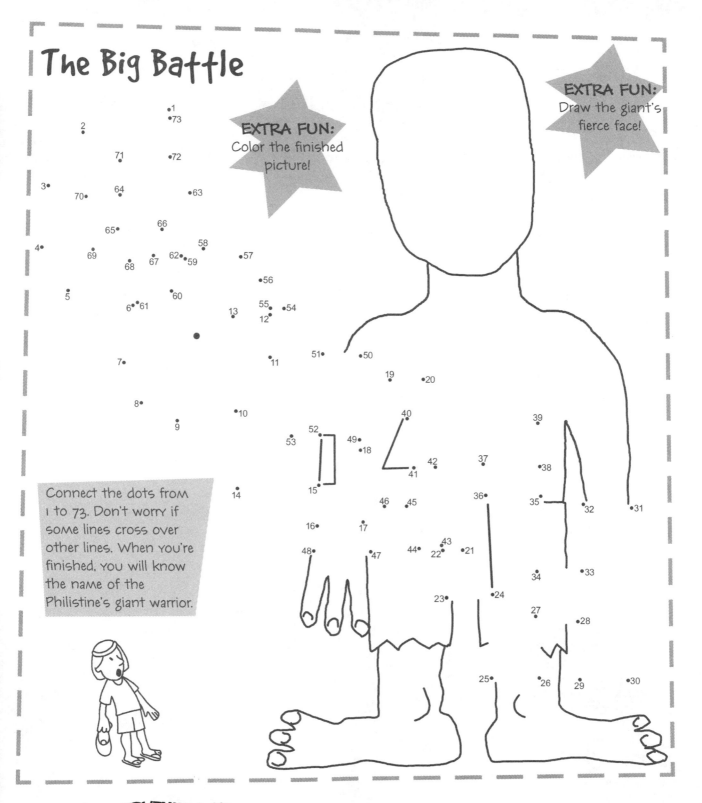

EXTRA FUN: Color the finished picture!

EXTRA FUN: Draw the giant's fierce face!

Connect the dots from 1 to 73. Don't worry if some lines cross over other lines. When you're finished, you will know the name of the Philistine's giant warrior.

David Becomes King

1. How did David feel when he heard that King Saul and his son Jonathan had died?
   a. He was happy
   b. He was lonely
   c. He was sad
   d. He didn't care

2. What land did David ask the Lord about?
   a. Judah   c. Moab
   b. Edom   d. Egypt

3. What happened to David when he arrived in the city of Hebron?

4. Who was proclaimed king of all of Israel by Saul's army captain?

5. Did the two kingdoms agree to get along?

6. What did the elders of Israel finally remember?

7. How did David feel they had won their battles?

8. When David went to fight the Philistines, what did God tell him?

9. Later, David would bring something into the tabernacle. What was it?
   a. The Ark of the Lord
   b. Philistine soldiers
   c. The Bible
   d. Candles

10. When David offered to build a house for the ark, what did the Lord say?

11. What happened to David when he married Bathsheba?

12. Did the Lord eventually forgive him?

Who Am I?

I am Abraham's nephew. I spent a lot of time fighting God's will and ways. My wife became a pillar of salt when she would not listen to God. **Who am I?**

Lot

blessing: The Lord gave His blessing to many of the people in the Bible. They were blessed with children, food, and happiness. Parents also gave their blessings or good wishes to their children. Today, people continue to use blessings in their daily lives.

Words to Know

A House of Worship

1. Bathsheba wanted one person to inherit King David's throne. Who was it?

2. Someone else wanted him to become king too; do you know who it was?

3. When David appointed Solomon to rule over two countries, which ones did he choose?
   a. Ammon and Gilead
   b. Israel and Judah
   c. Syria and Edom
   d. Gilead and Edom

4. What did Solomon and the people of Jerusalem feel they should build?

5. When Solomon spoke to the Lord, how did the Lord appear?
   a. In a vision
   b. In a dream
   c. As an angel
   d. In a fire

6. What did Solomon ask God to give him?

7. How did he demonstrate his wisdom?

8. What did Solomon plan to use to build the Lord's house?
   a. Cedar and stone
   b. Oak and bricks
   c. Apple-wood and goatskins
   d. Concrete and paper

9. How was the wood Solomon used decorated?
   a. With gold
   b. With carved flowers
   c. With carved cherubim
   d. All of the above

10. The room built to house the ark contained two statues; what were they?
    a. Golden lions
    b. Lambs
    c. Cherubim
    d. Moses and David

11. What did the Lord want Solomon to do?

12. After the ark was placed in the tabernacle of the Lord, what happened?

TRY THIS

▶ A Geography Lesson

Look at a map of the Middle East and see if you find Israel and Jerusalem. Does the map tell you the longitude and latitude of the area? Now can you find the longitude and latitude for the area where you live? Compare the two. Can you tell how far away you live?

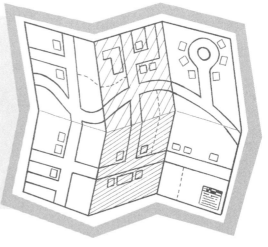

A Feast in the Wilderness

1. Why was the Lord displeased with King Ahab of Israel?

2. When Ahab married Jezebel, whom did he worship?
   a. Molech
   b. The devil
   c. Baal
   d. No one

3. Where did the Lord tell Elijah to hide so that he could drink?
   a. By a brook
   b. By a well
   c. By a river
   d. By a village

4. What kind of birds brought Elijah his food?
   a. Doves
   b. Ravens
   c. Eagles
   d. Parrots

5. Why did Elijah have to move?

6. Where did the Lord send Elijah next?

7. Why did she say that she couldn't help him?

8. How long did Elijah tell her that the Lord would provide food for them?

9. Why did the woman blame Elijah for her trouble?

10. What did Elijah ask the Lord to do?

11. When the child came back to life, what did the mother say?

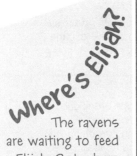

Where's Elijah?

The ravens are waiting to feed Elijah. But where is he hiding? Look closely to see if you can find him in this landscape.

Chapter 6 Answer Key

The Sun Stands Still
1. He and his army marched on to Ai
2. c. The people of Gibeon
3. The Amorites
4. He was at Gilgal
5. a. At dawn
6. a. Hailstones
7. To make the sun stand still over Gibeon
8. d. One day
9. Israel
10. No

The Weak Become Strong
1. So the children of Israel would return to God
2. b. They took their food
3. a. A prophet
4. The angel of the Lord
5. He had abandoned them
6. To know that he was really talking to God
7. The angel of the Lord brought fire from a rock
8. It was made for the idol Baal
9. b. 32,000
10. That they saved themselves
11. c. 300 men
12. Gideon won the battle

The Strength of Samson
1. After they lost their leader, they forgot about God
2. No
3. c. Let anyone cut his hair
4. The Philistines
5. a. A riddle
6. Samson's wife told them
7. b. The jawbone of a donkey
8. They offered Delilah silver if she would trick Samson into telling her
9. Delilah cut his hair while he slept
10. To offer him to their God
11. He moved the pillars that held the roof up

Ruth's Promise
1. b. A famine
2. She heard that the Lord had provided food for her people in the land of Judah
3. c. Food
4. To stay in Moab and find new husbands
5. c. At first they both chose to go, but one changed her mind
6. "Where you go, I will go"
7. That they would have the same people and the same God
8. b. By gleaning fields
9. d. Boaz
10. Because she left her homeland to help Naomi
11. To marry him
12. David

A King of Hearts
1. Choosing Saul as a King
2. So that Samuel could see the person chosen to be the new king
3. a. A heifer
4. God
5. The Lord did not look at the outside of a man, but at the inside
6. His heart
7. b. Tending the sheep
8. "Rise and anoint him, he is the one"
9. The Spirit of the Lord
10. a. Ill
11. b. A harp

The Giant
1. c. In the hills of Israel
2. b. Goliath
3. Over nine feet tall
4. A shield
5. d. Forty
6. The losers would serve the winners
7. They were worried
8. Out in the field to tend the sheep
9. To bring his brothers food
10. He challenged the army of the living God
11. He told Saul he had fought terrible beasts who had threatened his sheep
12. c. They ran away

David Becomes King
1. c. He was sad
2. a. Judah
3. He was anointed king of Judah
4. Ish-Bosheth, Saul's son
5. No, they had many battles
6. That the Lord had made David king
7. With the help and blessings of the Lord
8. That He would go ahead of him
9. a. The Ark of the Lord
10. That He wanted one of David's children to build it
11. He angered the Lord and was punished
12. Yes

A House of Worship
1. Her son Solomon
2. Adonijah
3. b. Israel and Judah
4. A house for the Lord
5. b. In a dream
6. An understanding heart to judge with
7. He used a test
8. a. Cedar and stone
9. d. All of the above
10. Cherubim
11. Keep His commandments
12. The glory of God filled the house

A Feast in the Wilderness
1. He was the most evil king the Hebrews had ever had
2. c. Baal
3. a. By a brook
4. b. Ravens
5. With no rain, the brook dried up and he had no water
6. To a woman in Zarephath
7. Her family had no food
8. Until it rained again
9. Her son died of thirst and hunger
10. To return the child's life
11. She knew Elijah was a man of God

One True God

Words to Know

1. Why did King Ahab and Obadiah search Samaria for water and grass for their animals?

2. What did the Lord tell Elijah to do?

3. When Elijah met Obadiah, why did he think he would help him?

4. How had Obadiah helped the Lord?

5. Why was Obadiah afraid to tell Ahab that Elijah was there?

6. When the rain did not come, whom did Ahab blame for Israel's troubles?
   a. Jezebel   c. God
   b. Elijah   d. Himself

7. Elijah blamed someone else for all of the problems. Who was it?
   a. Obadiah   c. The Philistines
   b. Ahab   d. Himself

8. What did Elijah tell Ahab to do?

9. When Elijah told the Hebrews that they must choose to follow either the Lord or Baal, what did they say?

10. God and Baal were supposed to provide something at the sacrifice—what was it?
   a. Lightning c. Animals
   b. Rain   d. Fire

11. What happened to Baal's prophets when he gave them no fire?

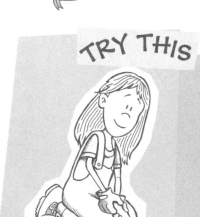

TRY THIS

▶ *Rained Out*

One way to measure rain is with a rain gauge. If you don't have one of your own, why not make it? Gather the following things: A clear plastic cup, a permanent marker, a dowel (or large stick), several rubber bands, and a ruler. Measure and mark your cup with inch lines, push your dowel into the ground, in your yard, and connect the cup to the dowel with rubber bands. Now all you need is rain!

Chariot of Fire

1. Who was the Samarian king, the son of Ahab and Jezebel, who reigned after his father's death?
   a. Jehoshaphat
   b. Asa
   c. Methuselah
   d. Ahaziah

2. After the king was injured, he sent his messengers to ask a god if he would recover. Which god was it?
   a. Baal-Zebub   c. Molech
   b. The Lord   d. Baal

3. Who told the king that a man had said he would not recover?

4. When the messengers told the king about the man, who did the king think he was?
   a. Elisha   c. Elijah
   b. Jonah   d. Ahab

5. Because Ahaziah sent armies to bring Elijah to him, what did God do?

6. What happened to the king after God sent Elijah to speak to him?
   a. He left the country
   b. He went to prison
   c. He died
   d. He became more powerful

7. Who was the prophet God chose to serve after Elijah?

8. While Elijah and Elisha were traveling, whom did they meet?

9. What did the prophets ask Elisha?

10. As Elijah struck the Jordan River with his cloak, something happened. What was it?

11. When the flaming chariot appeared and took Elijah up in a whirlwind, where did it take him?
    a. Heaven   c. Bethel
    b. Gilgal   d. Jericho

Who Am I?

I was not sure I wanted to be King the day I was chosen. But when God wanted David to succeed me, I became jealous and wanted to remain the king after all. If only I had listened more to God. **Who am I?**

Saul

An Ancient Vehicle

Chariots date back to ancient days, when their riders needed protection in a war or a way to go fast (as in a race). Chariots could be found in parades or processions of royalty or champions. In a way, chariots were the ancient versions of modern cars.

Fun Fact

A Room near the Sky

1. Where did Elisha go?
   a. To Jerusalem
   b. To Egypt
   c. To Jordan
   d. To Shunem

2. What did the woman ask the prophet to do when he passed by her house?
   a. To talk about God
   b. To drink some water
   c. To keep going
   d. To stay for a meal

3. What did the prophet do?

4. What did the woman tell her husband about the prophet?
   a. That he was a beggar
   b. That he was a Scribe
   c. That he was a man of God
   d. That he was a stranger

5. What did the couple decide to do for Elisha?

6. What did Elisha ask the Shunammite woman?

7. What problem did the woman have?

8. Was the woman's problem solved?

9. What happened to the boy?

10. Why was the mother upset?

11. When he came into the room, the child was no longer alive. What did Elisha do?

12. What happened next?

TRY THIS

▶ **Crown Yourself King**

Have you ever wanted to wear a crown, or at least try one on? With all that metal and all those jewels, you may grow tired of having that much weight on your head. But don't worry, you can practice walking around with something on your head, like a book or a plastic bowl. The fun part is having a relay to see who can go the longest with their "crown" still on.

Room Service

One of these houses has a room prepared for the prophet Elisha. Which house is it?
Cross out words according to the rules and you will find out!
Cross out the following kinds of words:

- Two-syllable words beginning with F
- Words with a double S
- Words that rhyme with SON
- Words that end in the letters AY
- Words that begin with the letter C

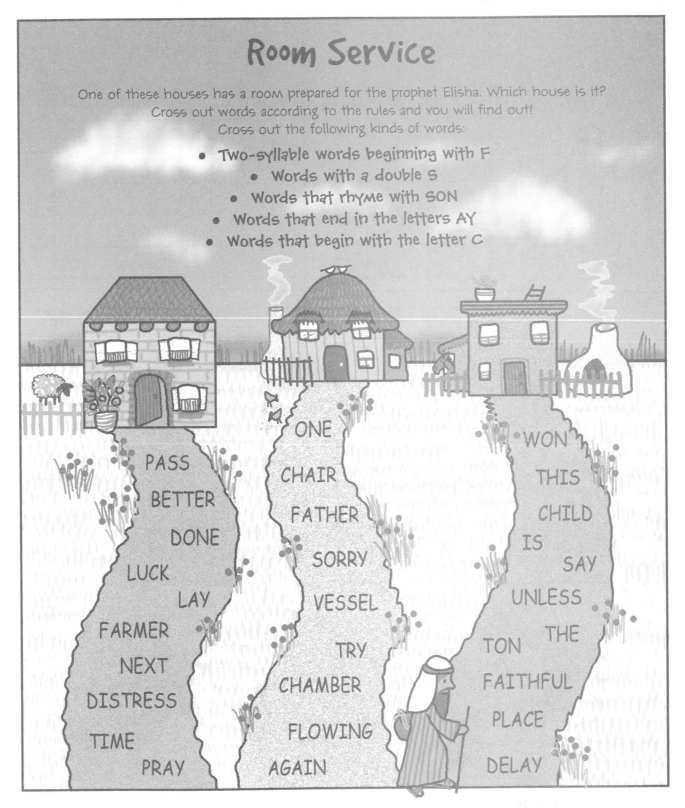

PASS
BETTER
DONE
LUCK
LAY
FARMER
NEXT
DISTRESS
TIME
PRAY

ONE
CHAIR
FATHER
SORRY
VESSEL
TRY
CHAMBER
FLOWING
AGAIN

WON
THIS
CHILD
IS
SAY
UNLESS
THE
TON
FAITHFUL
PLACE
DELAY

It's Official

When the palace guards surrounded Joash to protect him, what did the priest do?

Color the squares with a dot in the upper right corner to find out. Break the code at the bottom of the page and fill in the boxes with the correct letters, and you'll know for sure!

G+1	C+2			S-3	M-1	D-3	A+2	D+1	H-4	
E-4		F-3	Q+1	Q-2	T+3	T-6			M+2	M+1
J-2	A+8	W-4		P-8	B+3	B-1	A+3		

The Young King

1. When King Ahaziah died, who wanted to be ruler of the kingdom?

2. Who hid Ahaziah's son so that he might someday be king?
   a. Ahaziah's uncle
   b. Ahaziah's aunt
   c. Ahaziah's sister
   d. Ahaziah's friends

3. How long was the boy hidden from his grandmother?
   a. One year   c. Six years
   b. Five years d. Ten years

4. Where did the priest make a covenant with the palace guards?

5. After the guards were sworn by an oath, what did the priest do?

6. What did the people do when the boy was crowned and anointed king?
   a. They clapped their hands
   b. They said "Long live the king!"
   c. They did both
   d. They did nothing

7. When the queen heard the noise and entered the temple, what did she see?

8. How did she react to the crowning?

9. What musical instruments did the people play as they rejoiced over the new king?

10. How old was the young king when he began his reign?

oath: An oath is a vow or pledge. Giving an oath is one way to give someone your word or promise. God shared many oaths and vows with people in the Bible.

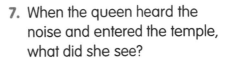

Words to Know

King of Kings

There are kings everywhere. Kings in palaces, kings in storybooks, kings in checkers, and kings in chess. You can play King of the Hill or King of Hearts. We have king-sized candy bars, and king-size beds. The most famous king of all though, was the King of the Jews, Jesus.

Fun Fact

Washed Clean

Who Am I?

I could have worked in the circus as a lion tamer—if I was sure my guardian angel would always be there. I wasn't very scared in the den. **Who am I?**

Daniel

1. What terrible illness did Naaman, the head of the Syrian King's army, have?
   a. Dropsy
   c. Leprosy
   b. Palsy
   d. Smallpox

2. Where was his wife's maid born?
   a. Israel
   c. Egypt
   b. Edom
   d. Judah

3. Why did the maid want Naaman to see the prophet from her country?

4. How did the king of Aram offer to help?

5. What did the letter ask of Israel's king?

6. The king of Israel was scared to help. Why?
   a. He did not want to catch leprosy
   b. He knew he wasn't God and thought if he failed they would quarrel with him
   c. He was afraid of their god
   d. He was afraid the Lord would disapprove

7. Why did Elisha want Naaman to see him?

8. Elisha sent Naaman a messenger. What was the messenger supposed to say?

9. Did Naaman go back to Syria after he washed in the river?

10. What did he say to Elisha?

11. When Elisha refused the gift, what did his servant do?

12. What happened to the servant?
    a. He got sick with Naaman's leprosy
    b. He became a king
    c. He became a rich man
    d. Elisha punished him for being greedy

Q. What is the best way to get to Paradise?

A. Turn right and stay straight.

Music of the Lord

1. Which of these names are in the Semites' family tree?
   - a. Noah
   - c. Shem
   - b. Isaac
   - d. All of the above

2. Who placed the Levites in the service of song in God's house?

3. Where did they sing for the congregation?

4. Who asked that the sons of Levi do different types of service for the tabernacle?
   - a. God
   - c. David
   - b. Moses
   - d. Noah

5. Who else tended the altars?

6. How were the Levites paid for the work they did for the Lord?
   - a. With food
   - b. With animals
   - c. With cities
   - d. All of the above

7. What else were the Levites given?

8. Who took care of the "city of refuge"?
   - a. The guards
   - b. The soldiers
   - c. The Levites
   - d. The accused themselves

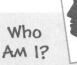

Who Am I?

I am well known as the one who betrayed Jesus. I was one of the twelve disciples who shared in the Last Supper of the Lord. Through prophecy Jesus knew I was the one who would give him away and seal his fate. **Who am I?**

Judas

Fun Fact

Ancient Melodies

Music may be one of the oldest arts. Instruments for making music have been found dating back thousands of years before Christ. Once people could speak, they soon learned to sing. In the Bible, there are many stories of people playing music for the Lord.

Why couldn't they play cards on the ark?

Noah was sitting on the deck!

The Gatekeepers

1. Where did the people of Judah and the other tribes of Israel settle when they returned from Babylon?

2. How many priests came back to work in the service of the Lord?
   a. Less than 1,200
   b. 1,200
   c. 1,700
   d. More than 1,700

3. The gatekeepers came from what tribe?
   a. Levi   c. Judah
   b. Benjamin d. Reuben

4. What were the duties of the gatekeepers?

5. How were they chosen?
   a. By Samuel
   b. By David
   c. By their rank of tribe
   d. All of the above

6. What did the chief gatekeepers take care of in the house of God?

7. Who was allowed to assist the gatekeepers?

8. Why did the gatekeepers live so close to the house of God?

9. What did the Levites have to watch over?

10. What did they prepare every Sabbath?

11. Why were the musicians for the Lord not responsible for any other work?

Sabbath Cake

Here is your chance to make your own Sabbath cake. In a bowl, mix together ½ cup of sugar and ½ cup of margarine, to that mixture add 1 egg, ¾ cup of flour, ¾ teaspoon of baking powder, ⅛ teaspoon of salt, ½ teaspoon of vanilla, and ⅓ cup of milk. Then pour your batter into a greased pan and bake at 350 degrees until the cake turns light brown. You can top your cooled cake with fruit or icing. For a really creative touch, decorate it with angels.

Gifts for the Temple

1. What did King David tell the men of Israel he planned to do?

2. Why did the Lord say He did not want David to build a house for His name?

3. Who did the Lord choose to build His house?
   a. Joash
   b. Solomon
   c. Asa
   d. All of the above

4. What did the Spirit of the Lord give to David, so he would know how to build the house?

5. Who was to carry out the work of building the house?

6. What else did the plans tell in great detail?

7. What had David gathered for the construction of the building?
   a. Marble   c. Jewels
   b. Wood   d. All of the above

8. Which part of the house did David say should be covered with silver and gold?

9. What other things were to be made out of silver and gold?

10. David asked all the people to give something. What was he hoping to receive?

11. How did David describe "our days on the earth"?
    a. Like a shadow
    b. Like sand in an hourglass
    c. As fleeting
    d. As long as eternity

12. Why did he say he and his people were so willing to give their time and wealth?

Who Am I?

My weakness and my strength were hidden in my hair. I liked to make others try to guess my riddles. My life was devoted to God, who gave me the strength everyone saw. **Who Am I?**

Samson

TRY THIS

▶ Here's a Riddle

Want to write your own riddle? It may be easier to start with the answer first. For example, if the answer is, "I am a raccoon," the riddle could be: "Why do I wear a mask all day when I have nothing to hide?" Now see if your friends can guess your riddle or make up one of their own.

The Ark of Zion

1. What did King Solomon buy in Egypt?
   a. Carts and cattle
   b. Boats and sheep
   c. Wheelbarrows and dogs
   d. Chariots and horses

2. When King Solomon was looking for someone to work with stone and metal, who did he ask for workers?
   a. The king of Tyre
   b. The king of Ammon
   c. The king of Midian
   d. The king of Egypt

3. What else did Solomon ask the man to do?

4. How many strangers did Solomon hire to work on the house?
   a. More than 15,000
   b. More than 2,000
   c. More than 150,000
   d. More than a million

5. Where did Solomon plan to build the house?

6. How tall were the pillars in front of the temple?
   a. Eighteen cubits
   b. Thirty cubits
   c. Sixty cubits
   d. Ninety cubits

7. What did Huram the craftsman create below the Sea?

8. When Solomon wanted to decorate the house, what did he use?

9. What did Solomon bring into the house when it was done?

10. Who watched the Levites bring the ark out of Zion?

11. What did the priests place under the wings of the cherubim before they left the Holy Place?

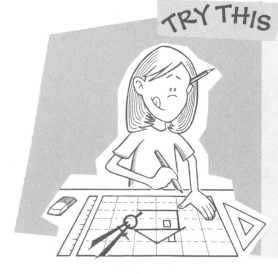

TRY THIS

▶ *A Cracker House*

Just like Solomon constructed a house for the Lord, you can build a house for yourself! All you need is a box of graham crackers and a container of frosting. It is easiest to build your house on a cookie sheet, using frosting to hold the foundation and your "walls" in place. You may also use other types of snacks as support from the inside. The best part is, after you're done, you can eat your creation!

Royal Raft

King Solomon is building a magnificent temple, and has ordered cedar, cypress, and algum timber from the city of Lebanon. The wood will be floated in rafts by sea to Joppa. Solomon has sent men to camp on the beach to carry the wood when it arrives. But which is the correct beach? Follow the directions and use the compass to figure out which is the beach at Joppa.

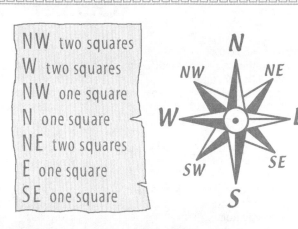

NW	two squares
W	two squares
NW	one square
N	one square
NE	two squares
E	one square
SE	one square

START

Chapter 7 Answer Key

One True God

1. There was a famine
2. Find Ahab and tell him that there would be rain again
3. Obadiah had helped God before
4. He had hidden God's prophets from the wrath of Jezebel, Ahab's wife
5. He was afraid Elijah would leave
6. b. Elijah
7. b. Ahab
8. Gather Baal's prophets and the people of Israel
9. They said nothing
10. d. Fire
11. They called out in vain to Baal

Chariot of Fire

1. d. Ahaziah
2. a. Baal-Zebub
3. The messengers
4. c. Elijah
5. He sent fire from Heaven to stop them
6. c. He died
7. Elisha
8. Prophets from all of the cities
9. If he knew his master was leaving him that day
10. The river divided and they crossed over dry ground
11. a. Heaven

A Room near the Sky

1. d. To Shunem
2. d. To stay for a meal
3. He stopped to eat
4. c. That he was a man of God
5. They offered him a small room upstairs to stay in
6. If there was something that he could do for her
7. She could not have children
8. Yes, she had a baby boy
9. His head was hurt and then he died
10. She asked why he would give her a son only to take him away
11. He prayed to God and touched the boy
12. The boy sneezed seven times and opened his eyes

The Young King

1. His mother
2. c. Ahaziah's sister
3. c. Six years
4. In the house of the Lord
5. He showed them the king's son
6. c. They did both
7. The newly crowned king
8. She told them it was treason
9. Trumpets
10. He was seven years old

Washed Clean

1. c. Leprosy
2. a. Israel
3. She thought Elisha could cure Naaman's leprosy
4. By sending a letter to Israel's king, offering a great reward in exchange for helping Naaman
5. To cure Naaman
6. b. He knew he wasn't God and thought if he failed they would quarrel with him
7. To prove that there was a prophet in Israel
8. That Naaman should wash himself seven times in the Jordan River and that would cure the leprosy
9. No, he went to see Elisha
10. He wanted to give Elisha a gift
11. He followed Naaman and asked for some of the gift
12. a. He got sick with Naaman's leprosy

Music of the Lord

1. d. All of the above
2. King David
3. In the tabernacle
4. a. God
5. Moses' brother Aaron and his sons
6. c. With cities
7. The suburbs around the cities, which were pastures for their flocks
8. c. The Levites

The Gatekeepers

1. "On their own property in their own towns"
2. d. More than 1,700
3. a. Levi
4. They guarded the house of God
5. d. All of the above
6. The rooms and the treasuries
7. Their families
8. It was their job to open the gates each morning
9. The instruments, furniture, food, and the spices
10. A special bread
11. They were to be available to make music at any time of the day or night

Gifts for the Temple

1. Build a house for the Ark of the Covenant
2. Because David had fought in battles and shed blood
3. b. Solomon
4. Plans
5. The priests and the Levites
6. How much every lampstand, dish, and table should weigh
7. d. All of the above
8. The walls
9. Decorations from the craftsmen
10. Their treasures and their help
11. a. Like a shadow
12. They were returning these gifts from God

The Ark of Zion

1. d. Chariots and horses
2. a. The king of Tyre
3. To buy wood from Lebanon
4. c. More than 150,000
5. In Jerusalem
6. a. Eighteen cubits
7. Twelve brass bulls
8. Gold
9. David's treasure
10. The elders of Israel
11. The Ark of the Covenant

A Time of Change

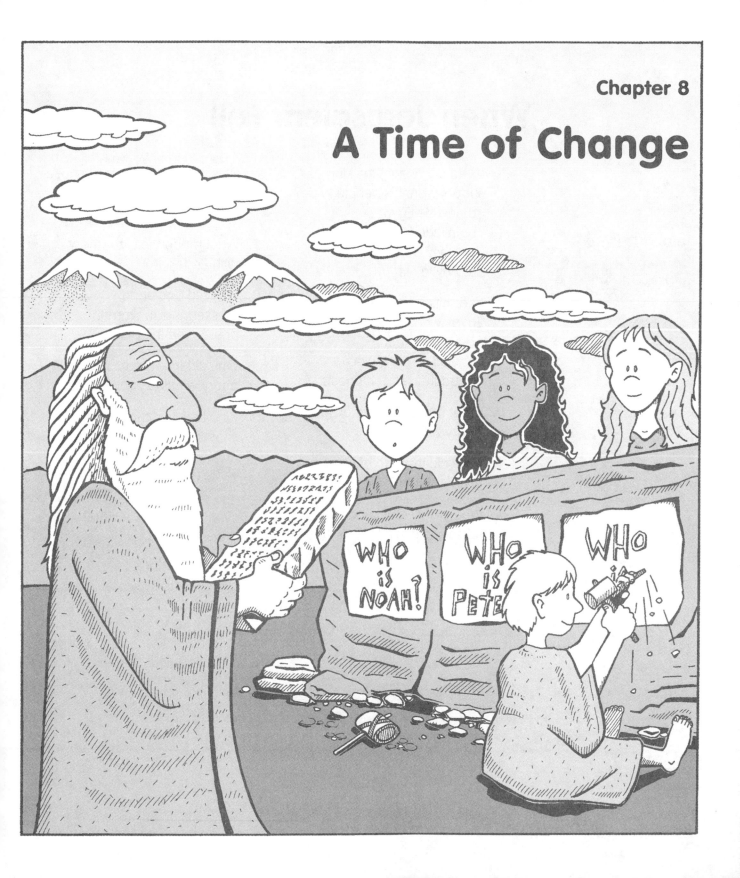

When the people of Jerusalem end their belief in God, Jerusalem comes to an end. —2 Chronicles 34:31–36:23

When Jerusalem Fell

judge: To decide or assess a problem. A judge must choose between two or more sides to make a final decision. In the Bible, God judges many people by their hearts and their actions.

Words to Know

1. What did Josiah, the king of Judah, want his people to do?
   a. Invade Egypt
   b. Invade Babylon
   c. Obey God
   d. Pay taxes

2. In addition to the king of Egypt, who else wanted peace with Judah?
   a. God   c. Molech
   b. Baal   d. The priests

3. What made the king of Egypt angry with Josiah?

4. How did the king of Egypt get even with him?

5. Where did Nebuchadnezzar take Jehoiachin?

6. When Nebuchadnezzar chose someone new for the king of Judah, who did he pick?

7. What made the Lord angry with Zedekiah?

8. Why did God send messengers to warn the priests and the people?

9. Why did the Lord grow so angry with the people?

10. Who believed that God had chosen him to rebuild God's house in Jerusalem seventy years later?
    a. Jeremiah   c. Elijah
    b. Elisha   d. Solomon

The Golden Rule

Do you know what the Golden Rule is? According to Matthew 7:12, it's "do to others what you would have them do to you"—treat others as you want to be treated. Although the words of the Golden Rule may differ among different religions and cultures, many of us share this basic belief.

Esther's Letter

1. King Ahasuerus invited the nobles of his empire to attend a feast. Who else was invited?
   a. The priest
   b. The prophet
   c. His wife
   d. All of the above

2. Why did the king become very angry when she refused?

3. What was the king told to do?
   a. To issue a royal order to keep her away from him forever
   b. To ask her to apologize
   c. To ask her to leave the empire
   d. To ignore her refusal

4. When the officers went in search of a new wife for the king, who was one of the girls that was chosen?

5. Where did they take Esther?
   a. To a cave
   b. To an altar
   c. To the palace
   d. To the temple

6. When they took Esther to the palace, why did she not tell the king that she was a Jew?

7. What did Esther become?
   a. A maid   c. A spy
   b. A queen   d. A doctor

8. How did Mordecai save the king's life?

9. Because Haman disliked Mordecai, he made a plan to get rid of the Jews. How did he plan to do that?

10. How did Haman determine when the plan or decree would take effect?

11. Why was the decree changed?

12. Esther sent a letter that said all Jews should keep Purim each year. Why did she want them to do this?

Who Am I?

For years, I have been feared by man. Because of me man has suffered great pain and loss. In one single moment I changed the world forever. **Who am I?**

The serpent

How do we know Isaiah's parents were good business-people?

They both raised a prophet (profit)!

How did God keep the oceans clean?

With Tide!

Two Kinds of Figs

1. Whom did Nebuchad-nezzar carry away?
   a. The son of the king of Judah
   b. The king of Israel
   c. The king of Judah
   d. The prince of Israel

2. What did the Lord show Jeremiah after that?
   a. A basket of figs
   b. Two baskets of figs
   c. Three baskets of figs
   d. Four baskets of figs

3. Where were the baskets?
   a. In a garden
   b. In front of the temple
   c. By his house
   d. At the beach

4. How did Jeremiah describe the figs in the first basket?

5. What did the second basket contain?

6. Who did the Lord say the good figs were like?

7. What did the Lord promise them when they returned?

8. How did the Lord think this would change His people?

9. Who did He describe as bad figs, too rotten to be eaten?

Fig Bar Cookies

Fig bar cookies are easy to make. First, place 3/4 cup of moist dried figs in a pan filled with 1/3 cup of water and 1/3 cup of sugar; simmer, stirring until the mixture thickens. Turn off the heat and let your homemade fig paste cool. In a bowl, mix 1 cup of brown sugar, 1/2 cup of butter, 1 egg, 1 teaspoon of vanilla, 1 3/4 cup of flour, and 3/4 teaspoon of salt. Combine and then roll the dough out. Spread the fig paste over the dough, roll it up into a log shape, and put in the fridge to chill. Once cold, slice your roll into cookies about a 1/4-inch thick and place them on a cookie sheet to bake at 400 degrees for 10 minutes.

The Writing on the Wall

1. What did Belshazzar, the king of Babylon, host for his lords?

2. When the king took the gold and silver cups from God's house, what did he use them for?

3. Who did the Babylonians praise while they drank?
   a. The warriors
   b. Themselves
   c. The God of Israel
   d. The gods of gold and silver

4. Why was Belshazzar frightened at the banquet?

5. When his wise men could not read the message, who came to calm him?
   a. His priest
   b. His father
   c. His mother
   d. God

6. Who was called upon to read the message?

7. What did the king ask Daniel?

8. How did Daniel offer to help?

9. When Daniel read the message, what did he say caused Nebuchadnezzar to lose the kingdom God had given him?
   a. His mistakes
   b. His foolishness
   c. His illness
   d. His pride

The Golden Rule

The Golden Rule contains several words that speak of fair treatment to others. Although the words may vary from religion to religion, almost every faith asks its followers to act according to the spirit of this rule.

When you have correctly filled in the grid, you will know "The Golden Rule," too! The letters in each column go in the squares directly below them, but not necessarily in the same order. Black squares are the spaces between words.

	N			E	R		T			W X			
T	O	U		O	T U Y	D	S		Y G E			
X	H	E	M X	D H L T	O	H		Y A O U	T			
I	T	O	E W	O O E R	H	I	N	H A D O				
			V		Y				G ,			
					R		W					
Y			W	U			V					
	E				T			U .				

God saves Daniel and proves He protects those who believe in Him. —Daniel 6:1–26

Daniel and the Lions

1. Which king honored Daniel and gave him power over all of Babylon?
   a. Cyrus
   b. Belshazzar
   c. Darius
   d. George

2. Who tried to prove that Daniel had failed to perform his duties for the king?
   a. The king's other administrators
   b. The Queen
   c. Daniel's friends
   d. Darius's idols

3. Why did they want to cause a problem for Daniel?

4. What kind of decree did they ask the king to issue?

5. Did this decree stop Daniel's worship?

6. When people saw Daniel praying to God, what did they do?

7. How did the king feel after his men threw Daniel into the den?
   a. That it was the right thing to do
   b. He felt nothing
   c. He didn't know about it
   d. He was upset

8. What did Darius tell Daniel he hoped would happen to Daniel?

9. How would the king make sure no one helped Daniel?

10. What did they find in the morning after the stone was rolled away?

Taming Lions

Lions are fairly easy to train to do tricks. By the time they are two, they are ready to learn—as long as the trainer is careful and treats the lions well. As lions grow older and more ferocious, they become more dangerous to their trainers.

TRY THIS

▶ *Test Your Strength*

Are you strong or weak? To find out, hold a series of strength tests with your friends. Here's one test: Hold an object in your hand and keep your arm straight out, level with your shoulder. Time how long you can hold the object up before you get tired. Another test is to place your back against the wall and crouch down as if you are sitting on a chair. How long can you stay this way? You can also try a staring contest with a friend to see who can go the longest without blinking or laughing.

Fun Fact

The angels measure Jerusalem to see if there is room for all the people God will send. —Zechariah 1:1–2:13

Measuring Jerusalem

1. During the reign of Darius of Babylon, what prophet communicated with God and His angels?
   a. Hosea
   b. Gabriel
   c. Zechariah
   d. Joshua

2. What did the angels of the Lord find when they walked the Earth?

3. When the angels spoke to God, what did they want to know?

4. Did God stay angry at Jerusalem?

5. Now sad for Jerusalem, what did the Lord have planned for the city?

6. What did the four horns the angel showed to Zechariah represent?

7. When the four craftsmen came, what were they going to do?

8. Who was the man Zechariah saw with a measuring line in his hand?
   a. One of the carpenters
   b. An angel
   c. A Gentile
   d. Another prophet

9. What was he measuring?
   a. The length of Jerusalem
   b. The height of Jerusalem
   c. The width of Jerusalem
   d. The length and height of Jerusalem

10. Did the angel think Jerusalem's size would grow?

11. What did the Lord want His people to do?

12. When God comes to live among the people of Jerusalem, who will join them?

TRY THIS

▶ **Measuring Cubits**

Measure your room or your house using cubits. You can make a cubit ruler by cutting a strip of cardboard 1.8 inches—or 1 cubit—in length. Then try measuring your bed, your parents' cars, your leg, and so on. You could also try making a cubit-long sandwich and have a fifty-cubit running relay party. What other ancient measurements do you know? There may be some listed in your Bible.

Building in Jerusalem

Zechariah has 24 cubes. Which one of the towers pictured below can he build?

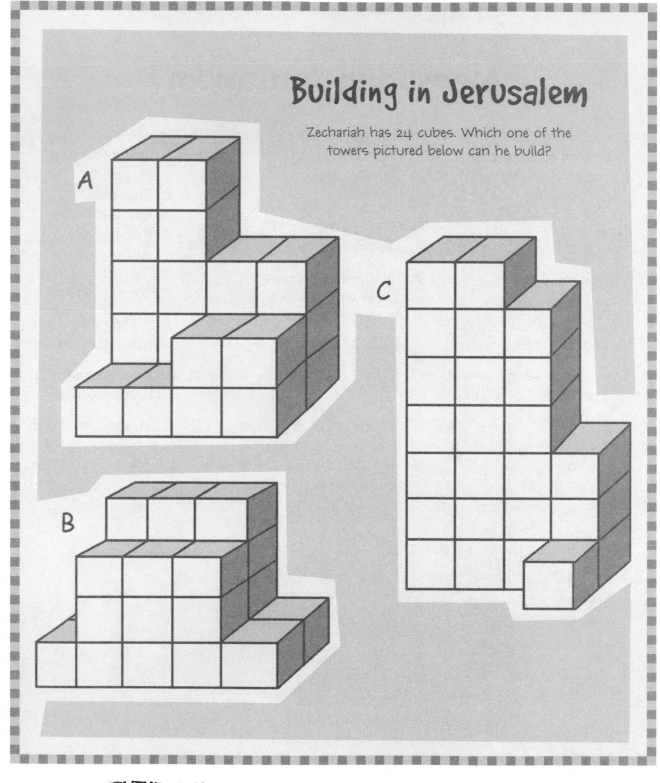

A

B

C

Of Shepherds and Angels

1. How many generations passed from Abraham to King David?
   a. Two
   c. Twelve
   b. Three
   d. Fourteen

2. When Jesus was born, how many generations had there been since David?
   a. Twenty-eight
   c. Fifteen
   b. Twenty
   d. Twelve

3. Who was Jesus' mother?

4. Who was Jesus' father?

5. When Joseph found out that Mary was with child, what happened next?

6. How did the angel come to see him?

7. Who was this child to be born of the Holy Spirit and of Mary?

8. What does *Immanuel* mean?

9. What did the angels say Mary and Joseph should call the child?

10. Had anyone expected these things to take place?

11. When speaking with Joseph, what did the angel say Jesus would do?

12. Where was Mary's baby born?
    a. Galilee
    c. Nazareth
    b. Bethlehem
    d. Jerusalem

Who Am I?

I was chosen by God to carry His child, the Son of Man. I rode by donkey to Bethlehem and stopped in a nearby stable. As a bright star shone above I gave birth to the Lamb of God. **Who am I?**

Mary

commandment: A rule, order, or law, such as the Ten Commandments that Moses received from God at Mount Sinai.

Words to Know

Our King Is Born

1. Who was the ruler of Jerusalem when the wise men searched for the newborn "king of the Jews"?
   a. Caesar   c. Philip
   b. Herod   d. Augustus

2. What did the wise men follow as they traveled to Bethlehem?
   a. A caravan   c. A star
   b. A comet   d. A map

3. How did Herod know where the child would be born?

4. Who did the prophet say would come from Bethlehem?

5. What did Herod ask the wise men?

6. Why did Herod say he wanted to find the child?

7. Where did the star lead the wise men?

8. What were the gifts the wise men brought for the baby?
   a. Gold
   b. Incense
   c. Myrrh
   d. All of the above

9. Why did the wise men decide not to return to Herod?

Where's the Star?

The three wise men didn't always have an easy time following the star that led to the town of Bethlehem. You won't have an easy time finding the five pointed star hiding in this puzzle, either!

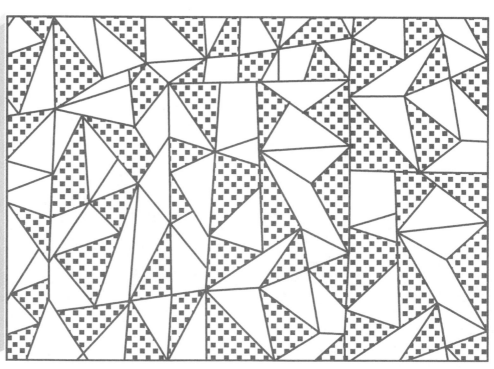

A Gift of Healing

1. When Jesus began to preach, why did he want the people to repent of their sins?

2. When Jesus met the two brothers, Simon (also known as Peter) and Andrew, what were they doing?
   a. Fishing in Galilee
   b. Herding sheep
   c. Hunting
   d. Working as carpenters

3. What did Jesus ask the two brothers to do?

4. Another set of brothers left their ship and followed him. What were their names?
   a. Matthew and Mark
   b. Judas and Luke
   c. James and John
   d. Matthew and John

5. How did Jesus begin bringing God's message to the people?

6. What were other ways he helped the people?

7. Were the people of Israel the only ones who had heard of Jesus?

8. What did Jesus say would happen to the poor in spirit?

9. What would the meek inherit?
   a. The Earth
   b. Rome
   c. Israel
   d. The universe

10. What did Jesus say about those who anger others by doing the right thing?

Who Am I?

When God commanded me to do His work, I hid in a boat. When a storm tossed me overboard, I was swallowed by a whale, and I stayed in the whale's belly until I decided to listen to God. **Who am I?**

Jonah

repent: To feel sorrow or remorse for what you have done. To ask for forgiveness and say you are sorry are ways to repent. God wanted His followers to repent for their bad behavior.

Our Closest Star

Our sun is one of the many stars in the universe, neither the smallest nor the largest. Even though the sun is our closest star, it's still over 90 million miles away from the Earth. It takes about 8 minutes for its warm rays to reach us—and that's a good thing! Sunlight is essential for life on Earth.

Fun Fact

Words to Know

Chapter 8 Answer Key

When Jerusalem Fell
1. c. Obey God
2. a. God
3. He helped some of his neighbors fight against Egypt
4. He invaded Judah and chose their next king
5. To Babylon
6. Zedekiah
7. He did evil and would not listen to the prophet Jeremiah
8. They were being unfaithful and not respecting the house of the Lord
9. They made fun of the prophets and God's words
10. a. Jeremiah

Esther's Letter
1. c. His wife
2. Because women were supposed to obey their husbands
3. a. To issue a royal order to keep her away from him forever
4. Esther, the cousin of Mordecai, a captured Jew
5. c. To the palace
6. Mordecai forbid it
7. b. A queen
8. He told Esther about a plot against the king
9. By tricking the king
10. By lot
11. The king realized the queen and her family were Jewish
12. To remember the day they were saved

Two Kinds of Figs
1. a. The son of the king of Judah
2. b. Two baskets of figs
3. b. In front of the temple
4. Good
5. Figs "so bad they could not be eaten"
6. The good people of Judah God had sent away
7. He would help them grow and let them stay there
8. They would return to Him with all their whole hearts
9. King Zedekiah and his people

The Writing on the Wall
1. A banquet
2. To drink wine
3. d. The gods of gold and silver
4. He saw someone's finger write a message on the wall
5. c. His mother
6. Daniel
7. If he was the exile his father brought out of Judah
8. He would read the writing and tell the king what it meant
9. d. His pride

Daniel and the Lions
1. c. Darius
2. a. The king's other administrators
3. They could not find his weakness
4. That anyone who prays to any god or man other than Darius for thirty days would be thrown into the lions' den
5. No
6. They went to King Darius
7. d. He was upset
8. That Daniel's God would deliver him from harm
9. By placing a stone in front of the den and sealing it with a ring
10. Daniel came out unharmed

Measuring Jerusalem
1. c. Zechariah
2. They found peace
3. When God's anger with Jerusalem and Judah would end
4. No
5. To rebuild God's house and bring back the people
6. Those who "scattered Judah, Israel, and Jerusalem"
7. Frighten the nations opposed to Judah
8. b. An angel
9. d. The length and height of Jerusalem
10. Yes
11. Return home
12. The other nations

Of Shepherds and Angels
1. d. Fourteen
2. a. Twenty-eight
3. Mary
4. Joseph
5. An angel came to see Joseph
6. In a dream
7. Jesus (Immanuel)
8. "God with us"
9. Jesus
10. Yes
11. He would save people from their sins
12. b. Bethlehem

Our King Is Born
1. b. Herod
2. c. A star
3. His chief priests and teachers told him
4. A ruler of Israel
5. When they had first seen the star
6. He said he wanted to worship the king
7. To the baby Jesus and his mother
8. d. All of the above
9. In a dream, God had warned them against it

A Gift of Healing
1. He said, "The kingdom of heaven is near"
2. a. Fishing in Galilee
3. To join him, and become fishers of men
4. c. James and John
5. By teaching in synagogues
6. He healed them
7. No; he had become known in other distant lands
8. They would be blessed
9. a. The Earth
10. "Theirs is the kingdom of heaven"

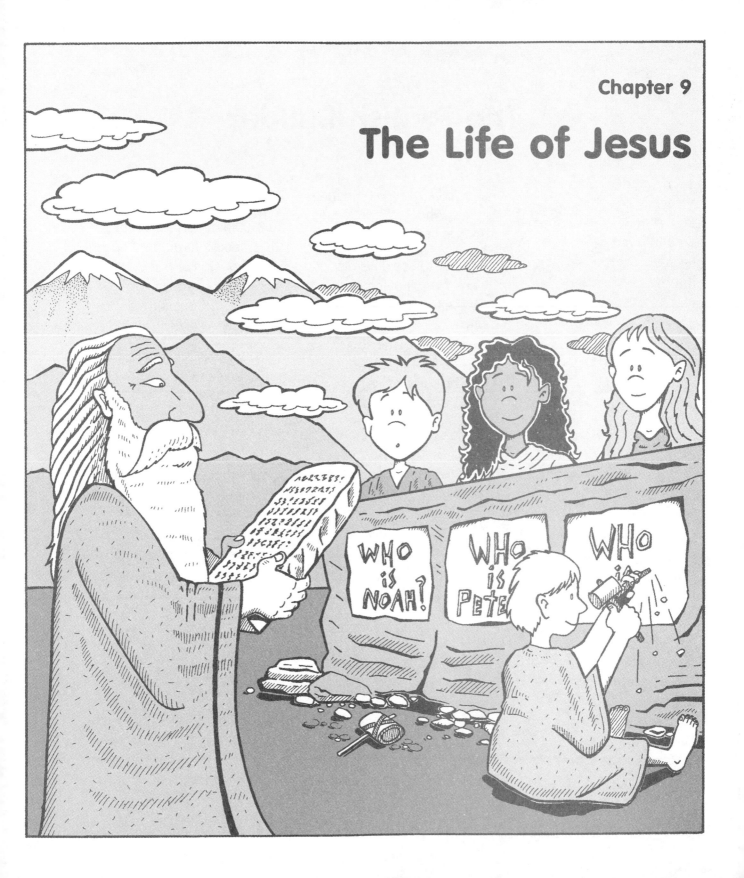

The Foolish Builder

sacrifice: To sacrifice something, you must give it up. In Biblical times, people offered sacrifices to God to show Him their love and commitment. God sacrificed His son to show His love and fulfill the prophecy.

Words to Know

Q. Where is the first baseball game in the Bible?

A. In the big inning. Eve stole first, Adam stole second, Cain struck out Abel, and the Prodigal Son came home.

1. Jesus said that his disciples should be glad to be persecuted. What explanation did he give them?

2. When Jesus said his disciples were the salt of the Earth, what else did he say they were?
   a. The salt of the soul
   b. The light of the world
   c. The spice of life
   d. The shadow of the valley

3. Did Jesus come to change the law of God's prophets?
   a. Yes   c. Most of them
   b. No   d. Some of them

4. Did Jesus accept the idea of "an eye for an eye"?

5. Did Jesus want everyone to love their neighbors?

6. How did Jesus feel about the people who were bad?

7. How did Jesus understand the Lord's Prayer?

8. Where did Jesus say it was foolish to gather treasure?
   a. On Earth
   b. In Heaven
   c. On treasure islands
   d. In castles

9. What is the law that speaks of being fair?

10. What people were like the man who built his house upon a rock?

11. Did anything happen to those who followed the laws?
   a. They earned respect
   b. They survived
   c. They had visions
   d. They were punished

12. How did Jesus feel about those who refused?

Not Knots

The foolish builder is one who builds his house on a foundation of sand. The same foolish builder is trying to tie some knots. Can you tell which knot will pull tight, and which knots will slip and slide apart when he pulls? Do you think these knots could be used to hold anything together?

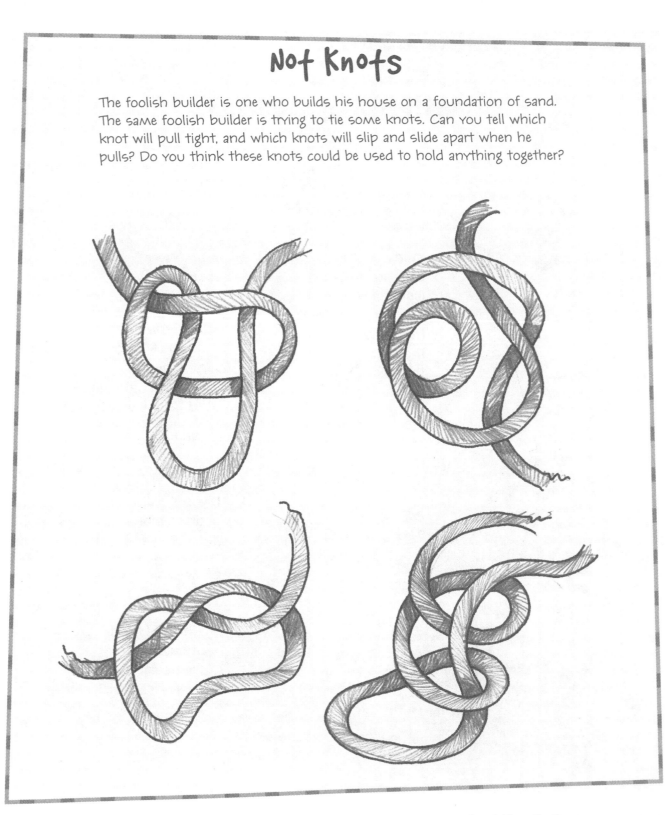

Walking on Water

Who Am I?

Even though I was very small, my faith was very big. With the help of God I beat the giant and became a king. God chose me for a king because of my good heart. **Who am I?**

David

1. After Jesus sent away the multitudes of people, what did he tell his disciples they should do?

2. Where did Jesus go?
   a. Out into the desert
   b. Up on a hill to pray
   c. Out in a small boat
   d. Down to the sea

3. What happened to his disciples?

4. Who came walking across the sea to them?

5. Why were the disciples afraid?

6. What message did Jesus give them?

7. Which disciple asked Jesus if he could try the same thing?
   a. Peter   c. Judas
   b. James   d. Matthew

8. How far did the disciple walk on the water?
   a. Halfway across the sea
   b. Fifty feet
   c. Until he started to sink
   d. All the way to shore

9. What caused him to sink?

10. How did Jesus save him?

11. What did Jesus say the disciple needed?
    a. A deep breath
    b. Confidence
    c. Faith
    d. All of the above

12. What did the disciples say about Jesus?
    a. He is the Messiah
    b. He is the Holy Ghost
    c. He is a nice guy
    d. He is the Son of God

Not a Foreign Language

Body language is the language of actions, motions, and expressions. We all use body language without realizing it. If you shrug your shoulders, you are saying "I don't know" with your body. If you roll your eyes, it's a sign you're upset or annoyed. People don't always need to rely on spoken language. In some Biblical stories, people have used body language, such as when Judas betrayed Jesus.

Fun Fact

Food for 5,000

1. What was another name for a disciple of Jesus?
   a. Angel
   b. Cherubim
   c. Apostle
   d. Prophet

2. Why did Jesus decide to take his disciples for a trip in a boat?
   a. They were surrounded by people
   b. They had no chance to rest
   c. They had no time to eat
   d. All of the above

3. Were they alone when they docked?

4. What did Jesus feel he should do with all the people gathered?

5. Why were the disciples worried?

6. What did the disciples think the people should do?

7. Instead, Jesus told his disciples to feed all the people. What did the disciples fear?

8. What did Jesus have them check?

9. When they handed him the food, what did he do next?

10. After Jesus blessed the food, what did he have the disciples do?

11. When Jesus fed the crowd of 5,000, he used five loaves of bread and what else?
    a. Two fish
    b. A lamb
    c. Five chickens
    d. Ten eggs

12. How many baskets of food were left when they had finished eating?
    a. Ten   c. Twenty
    b. Twelve   d. Thirty

TRY THIS

▶ A Picture Is Worth a Thousand Words

In the past, people often told stories from the Bible by painting them on a wall. Wall paintings are known as murals, and you can make one too—as long as your parents don't mind. You can use a large piece of paper or an old sheet taped to the wall. Then pick a scene from the Bible to draw or illustrate. Try using several different items like string, tube paint, and markers, just for fun.

food for 5,000

Many different kinds of people came to hear Jesus preach—and all of them were hungry! Can you find the following foods hiding in the crowd? HINT: Some of the foods are partially hidden behind people or other foods. PINEAPPLE, MUFFIN, ICE CREAM CONE, FRENCH FRIES, MUSHROOM SLICE, ORANGE SLICE, BACON STRIP, PIZZA SLICE, FISH, STRAWBERRY, CANDY CANE, BREAD SLICE, BAGEL, PIE SLICE, CARROT, BANANA, BUNCH OF GRAPES.

Jesus discusses John the Baptist's role in bringing the Word of God to the people. —Luke 7:16–34

Jesus' Friend John

1. When Jesus healed the people in the crowds, what did they call him?

2. How did John the Baptist hear of the wonders that Jesus was performing?
   a. From his disciples
   b. From Jesus' disciples
   c. From the crowds
   d. From God

3. What did John's disciples ask Jesus?

4. Why were the people happy to see Jesus?

5. Did Jesus believe that John was a prophet?
   a. Yes, and more
   b. No, not yet
   c. He was not sure
   d. No, he would never believe it

6. When Jesus said John was sent to prepare the way for him, what did he call John?
   a. A porter
   b. A messenger
   c. An elder
   d. A friend

7. What did the people baptized by John accept?

8. How did Jesus feel about the men of this time?

9. The people said they feared John. Why?

10. Why did they make fun of Jesus?

TRY THIS

▶ *What's in a Name?*

If you want to find out what your name means, you can look it up in a book at the library. You can also try to guess what your family and friends' names mean. When you meet someone new, see if you can guess what his or her name is before you are told. Does the name fit his or her appearance? You might ask your family how your name was chosen too. There is usually a story behind each person's name. If you look up Jesus' name, you will find it means "salvation."

Sowing Seeds

Who Am I?

I knew God as a child and also as an adult. I was a devoted follower of the Lord and tried to help Elijah in his work with the Lord. My name means "servant of God." **Who am I?**

Obadiah

1. How did Jesus preach the Good Word about the Kingdom of God?
   a. With psalms
   b. With parables
   c. With proverbs
   d. With pictures

2. What was one of the subjects of his parables?

3. What happened to the seeds lost by the wayside?

4. If other seeds fell upon a rock and received no moisture, what happened to them?

5. Did those seeds that drifted into a field of thorns do well?

6. When the seeds fell on good ground, what kind of harvest did they have?
   a. One of 100-fold
   b. One of 200-fold
   c. A good harvest
   d. A bad harvest

7. When the disciples heard the parable, what did they want Jesus to do?

8. How did Jesus explain what the seeds represented?
   a. The nation of Israel
   b. The Word of God
   c. Food for the crowds
   d. The disciples themselves

9. What did the seeds that fell by the wayside represent?

10. What are the seeds on the rock?

11. What are the seeds among the thorns?

12. What are the seeds growing on the good ground?

Biblical Geography

The events described in the Bible took place in the Middle East. Today, these lands are known as Israel, Syria, Egypt, Lebanon, Libya, Greece, Jordan, Ethiopia, and Turkey. Several of the rivers and mountains carry the same names they had during the times that Jesus walked the Earth.

Fun Fact

The Lost Sheep

1. Why were the Pharisees angry with Jesus?

2. How did Jesus teach the sinners?
   a. He preached long sermons
   b. He wrote on scrolls
   c. He told them parables
   d. He assigned readings to them

3. What did Jesus say about the shepherd who lost one sheep out of a flock of 100?

4. Jesus spoke of a woman who was missing only one of her coins. How did she feel when she found it?
   a. Safe   c. Happy
   b. Rich   d. Confused

5. In the parable of the father and son, what did the son ask of his father?

6. What happened to the son?
   a. He took the wealth
   b. He spent it all in another country
   c. He grew hungry
   d. All of the above

7. Why did he decide to return home?

8. How did his father feel?
   a. Happy to see him
   b. Disappointed
   c. Angry
   d. Annoyed

9. What did the father want to do for his son?
   a. Be happy
   b. Have a feast
   c. Have a dance
   d. All of the above

10. How did the eldest son feel when he heard that his father was so glad to see his brother?

11. What did the eldest son ask his father about his brother?

TRY THIS

▶ *Ancient Writings Recovered*

Want to impress your friends with an ancient-looking scroll? If you don't have one lying around, why not make one? All you need to do is write something (for instance, your own life story) on a long piece of paper, roll it up, and tie it with a fancy ribbon or string. Then, to make it look old, dip the edges in strong tea and let it dry on paper towels.

Jesus and the Little Children

1. When the people brought their babies for Jesus to touch, what did his disciples tell them?
   a. Not to go near him
   b. To wait
   c. To return another time
   d. To go away and never come back

2. Why did Jesus tell them to let the children come to him?

3. What did he say would happen if the people did not receive the Kingdom as a child?

4. Why did Jesus tell the rich ruler that he was not the "Good teacher"?

5. What did the ruler ask of Jesus?
   a. Wealth
   b. Friends
   c. Eternal life
   d. To be cured of leprosy

6. Did the ruler know the commandments?
   a. He did not know them
   b. He did not believe them
   c. He did know them but did not keep them
   d. He had kept them all of his life

7. What did Jesus tell the ruler he needed to do?

8. How did the ruler look when Jesus told him to give his wealth away?
   a. Sad   c. Brave
   b. Worried   d. Unworried

9. In what way did Jesus explain to the ruler how hard it would be?

10. What did Peter remind Jesus that the disciples had done?

11. Those who choose the Kingdom of God would receive what?

12. What did Jesus say would happen once they reached Jerusalem?

Jesus proves his power to his disciples. —John 1:51–2:11

Water to Wine

1. What does Jesus tell a man that he will see?

2. Where did Mary attend a marriage?
   a. Nazareth
   b. Cana of Galilee
   c. Bethlehem
   d. Jerusalem

3. When Jesus and his disciples came, what did Mary tell Jesus was missing?
   a. Bread
   b. Water
   c. Wine
   d. All of the above

4. Why did Jesus tell her he could not help her?

5. What did Mary ask of the servants?

6. When he was ready, what did Jesus ask for?
   a. Wine glasses
   b. Buckets
   c. Bowls
   d. Water jars

7. What liquid did they use to fill the jars?

8. Then Jesus told them to serve the liquid to someone. Who was it?
   a. The bride
   b. The groom
   c. The bride's family
   d. The master of the banquet

9. What did the master of the banquet say to the bridegroom?

10. Did the master of the banquet know where the wine came from?

11. What was the meaning of this event?

12. Why was this event so important?

Turn Water into Wine

You can perform your own wine miracle by turning water into pretend wine. First, get some powdered drink mix and put it in a pitcher (make sure you can't see through the pitcher, so that no one knows about the powder). When you are ready to amaze your friends, pour in the water, mix, and out will come a fruity drink. There are also several ways to make your pretend wine or punch better. Try adding two different flavors, or make pineapple ice cubes by freezing pineapple juice in ordinary ice-cube trays.

Transformers

It would be impossible for you to turn a glass of water into wine. However, it is very possible for you to turn a heart into a bird—or a fish, bug, or spaceship! Cross out each item in the "accessories" list as you use it to change each familiar shape into something completely different. Here's a sample bird.

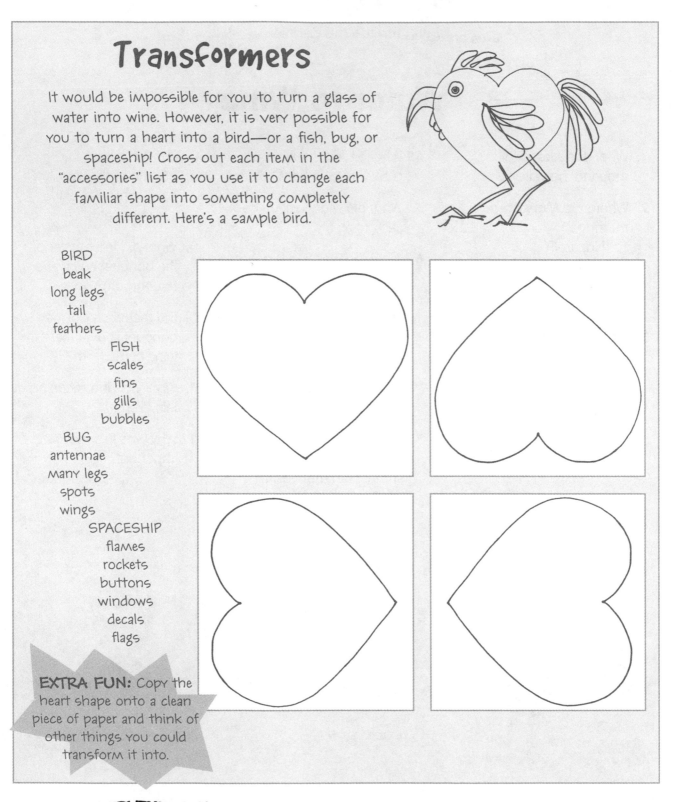

BIRD
beak
long legs
tail
feathers

FISH
scales
fins
gills
bubbles

BUG
antennae
many legs
spots
wings

SPACESHIP
flames
rockets
buttons
windows
decals
flags

EXTRA FUN: Copy the heart shape onto a clean piece of paper and think of other things you could transform it into.

Supper for the Lord

1. Why did Jesus gather his disciples together for supper?

2. Who encouraged Judas to betray Jesus?

3. When Jesus washed the disciples' feet, he said that not all of them were clean. What did he mean?
   a. One of them would betray him
   b. Their feet should be washed again
   c. He did not wash everyone's feet
   d. Washing feet wasn't enough

4. How did Jesus give his betrayer a sign?

5. After Judas left, what did Jesus ask the remaining disciples to do?

6. How many times did Peter deny Jesus before the morning came?
   a. One time   c. Three times
   b. Two times   d. Many times

7. What did Jesus tell his disciples he was going to do?
   a. Send them to Egypt
   b. Leave them money
   c. Prepare a place for them
   d. Go back to Nazareth

8. How could the disciples show they loved Jesus?

9. Why did God love the disciples?

10. Jesus asked his father to care for his disciples and hoped the world would believe what?

Who am I?

You may have heard of me in a parable. I am the beggar who meets the rich man. I was one of Jesus' friends along with my sisters. **Who am I?**

Lazarus

TRY THIS

▶ *What Are the Odds?*

Can you guess the odds of getting a particular number by tossing the dice? Try throwing dice many times and keep track of your results. Do you see a pattern? You can make you own set of dice by using empty ring boxes or larger square boxes. All you need is a box with six sides, each side having one more dot than the next, from one to six. Then toss your dice ten times with a friend and see who gets the highest score.

Chapter 9 Answer Key

The Foolish Builder

1. They would be rewarded in Heaven
2. b. The light of the world
3. b. No
4. No, he recommended turning the other cheek
5. Yes, and their enemies
6. That they share the same sun as people who are good
7. If you forgive others, God will forgive you
8. a. On Earth
9. "Do to others what you would have them do to you"
10. Those who listened to Jesus' sayings
11. b. They survived
12. They were foolish like the man who built his house upon the sand

Walking on Water

1. Take a boat out on the water
2. b. Up on a hill to pray
3. Their boat began to toss in the waves
4. Jesus
5. They thought he was a ghost
6. Not to worry
7. a. Peter
8. c. Until he started to sink
9. He was scared of the wind
10. He reached out his hand and caught him
11. c. Faith
12. d. He is the Son of God

Food for 5,000

1. c. Apostle
2. d. All of the above
3. The people went there to meet them
4. Teach them
5. There was nothing for the people to eat
6. Go and buy food for themselves
7. That it would cost too much to feed so many
8. How much food they had with them
9. He took the food and looked up to Heaven
10. Give it to the people
11. a. Two fish
12. b. Twelve

Jesus' Friend John

1. "A great prophet"
2. a. From his disciples
3. If he was the one predicted to come
4. He drove out their evil spirits and cured them
5. a. Yes, and more
6. b. A messenger
7. God's Word
8. That they were like children
9. Because he did not eat bread or drink wine
10. Because he did eat bread and drink wine

Sowing Seeds

1. b. With parables
2. The sower of seeds
3. They were eaten by the birds
4. They died
5. No, they were choked out
6. a. One of 100-fold
7. Explain the meaning of the parable
8. b. The Word of God
9. People who hear but the Devil takes the knowledge away
10. People who lose their faith
11. The followers lost to things of the Earth
12. Those who hear, obey, and teach God's Word

The Lost Sheep

1. He preached to the sinners
2. c. He told them parables
3. How happy he was when it was found
4. c. Happy
5. His inheritance
6. d. All of the above
7. He wanted to become a servant so he could eat
8. a. Happy to see him
9. d. All of the above
10. He became angry
11. If he liked the wandering son more than the son who had been loyal and stayed with him

Jesus and the Little Children

1. a. Not to go near him
2. Because the Kingdom of God belonged to them
3. They would never enter it
4. He said that no one is good but God
5. c. Eternal life
6. d. He had kept them all of his life
7. Give his wealth to others and follow him
8. a. Sad
9. He said it is easier for a camel to go through the eye of a needle
10. They had given up everything to follow him
11. Many blessings and everlasting life in the world to come
12. What the prophets have foretold

Water to Wine

1. Heaven will open and angels will be ascending and descending on the Son of Man
2. b. Cana of Galilee
3. c. Wine
4. He was not ready
5. To do whatever Jesus told them to do
6. d. Water jars
7. Water
8. d. The master of the banquet
9. That it was the best wine
10. No
11. It was the first miracle performed by Jesus
12. It showed Jesus' power and made his disciples believe in him

Supper for the Lord

1. He knew that he was going to leave this world
2. The devil
3. a. One of them would betray him
4. He gave him a piece of dipped bread
5. To love one another as he has loved them
6. c. Three times
7. c. Prepare a place for them
8. By keeping his commandments
9. Because they had loved Jesus
10. That he came from God

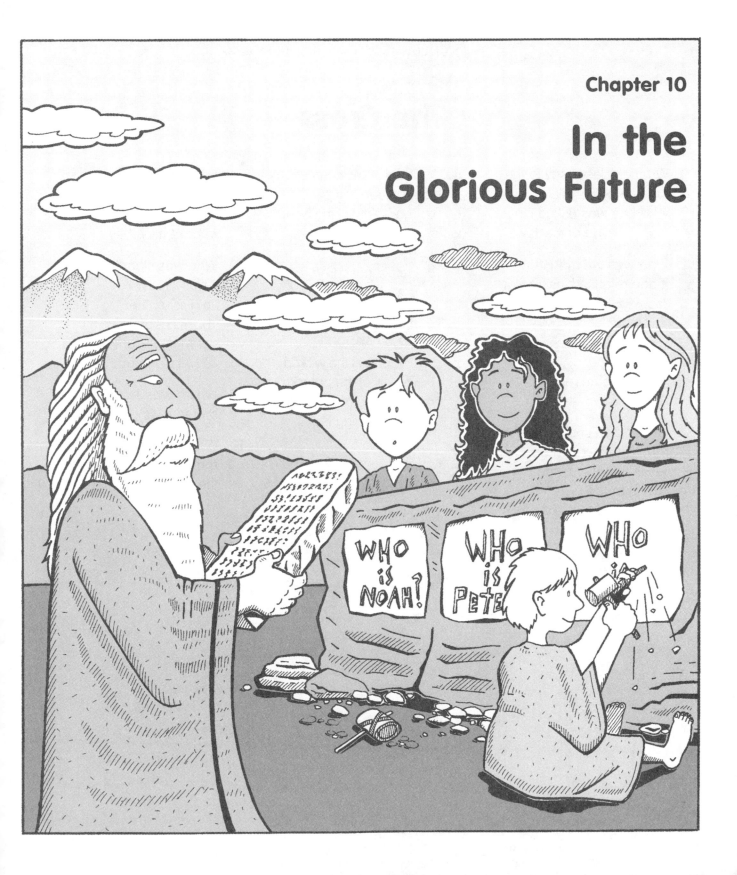

In the Glorious Future

The Cross

1. What did Jesus say to the judge, Pontius Pilate, when he was asked if he was the King of the Jews?

2. Who was the man the judge released instead of Jesus?
   a. Judas
   b. Peter
   c. Barabbas
   d. His name remains unknown

3. The Roman soldiers put a robe and a crown on Jesus. What was the crown made of?
   a. Flowers   c. Silver
   b. Thorns   d. Gold

4. What did Jesus carry on his shoulders?
   a. The weight of the world
   b. Guilt
   c. The cross
   d. He did not carry anything

5. What does *Golgotha* mean?
   a. The land of the wicked
   b. The hill of the unlucky
   c. The place of the skull
   d. The meaning is unknown

6. What was written on the sign Pilate placed on the cross?

7. When Jesus was carried away, how did the soldiers decide who was to have his robe?

8. Who was standing by Jesus' cross?
   a. His mother
   b. His aunt
   c. Mary Magdalene
   d. All of the above

9. Where was Jesus' mother invited to stay?

10. What promise had Jesus made before he went to the cross?

Cross Codes

Use the decoder below to answer the first question.
Break the code to the right to answer the second.

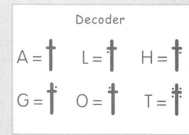

Decoder

A = †   L = †   H = †

G = †   O = †   T = ‡

The place where the soldiers took Jesus to be crucified:

† † † † † † † †

_ _ _ _ _ _ _ _

This is what the name means:

ETH _____

EACPL _____

FO _____

HET _____

KULSL _____

The Resurrection

1. Mary Magdalene came to the tomb on the first day of the week. What did she see?

2. When she found two disciples, what message did she give them?

3. Why were they surprised to learn he was gone?

4. Who did Mary see when she looked into the tomb?

5. What did he tell her?

6. Whom did Mary tell that she had seen Jesus?
   a. The disciples
   b. The priests
   c. God
   d. Everyone

7. When Jesus appeared that night, what did he ask them to receive?
   a. Wine
   b. Bread
   c. The Holy Spirit
   d. Water

8. One of the disciples was not there. What did he say when he heard the Lord was there?

9. What was this disciple's name?

10. When this disciple saw him, what did Jesus say?

11. What did Jesus share with his disciples when he appeared at the Sea of Tiberias?
    a. More parables
    b. New clothes
    d. Bread and fish
    d. All of the above

burden: A weight or responsibility one must carry or bear. Jesus had the burden of carrying his cross and the sins of the people of the world.

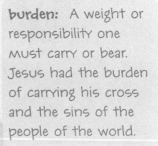

Words to Know

Egg Cave Toast

Some people eat egg caves during Easter because they represent the tomb or cave where Jesus was buried and arose three days later. But you don't need to wait for Easter to make an egg cave of your own. Take a piece of bread and use a round cookie cutter to press a circle out of the center. Then butter both sides of the bread and place it in an electric skillet or frying pan on medium heat. Add a raw egg into the hole of the grilling bread. After the first side is browned, turn your toast over and cook the other side. You can add cheese, meat, or other items if you like. If you cook the cut out circle you'll have an extra little piece of toast.

Peter's Escape

1. Which of the disciples was killed by Herod?
   a. Andrew   c. Peter
   d. Thomas   d. James

2. Whom did Herod put in prison?

3. What did Herod intend to do with this disciple after Passover?

4. How did the king keep him in prison?
   a. By soldiers
   b. By chains
   c. By guards at the door
   d. All of the above

5. Who helped free Peter from prison?

6. What did this individual do first?

7. What happened next?

8. Did Peter think the escape was real?

9. What happened when they reached the door to the outside?

10. According to Peter, who had delivered him from Herod's hands?

11. Where did Peter go after his escape?

12. What became of king Herod?

What animal could Noah not trust?

The cheetah!

Paul brings God's message and some rules to the Gentiles. —Acts 13:4–15:35

A Message from Paul

1. What was Saul (later known as Paul) doing in the synagogues?

2. Why did the Jews envy Paul?
   a. Many people came to hear him
   b. He was a friend of Pharisees
   c. He was from Syria
   d. He sounded important

3. What made Paul turn to the Gentiles to preach the Word of God?

4. Why did Paul say the Lord had sent them to the Gentiles?

5. When did Paul heal a man?

6. How did Paul travel from Attalia to Antioch?

7. When Paul and the disciples gathered at a church in Antioch, what did they say God had done?

8. Did Simon think God had a plan?

9. When the elders and apostles decide to send a letter to the Gentiles, where were they going to send it?
   a. Antioch
   b. Syria
   c. Cilicia
   d. All of the above

10. Did the work of the apostles affect the Church?

Paul's Message

Paul has written a letter to his friend Barnabas. However, since certain people have tried to keep Paul quiet and have even tried to kill him, Paul has written his message in code. Can you figure out how to read Paul's letter?

reetingsG!

etL su isitv uro rothersb ni verye ityc
herew ew aveh reachedp het ordw fo
het ordL nda ees owh heyt rea. eW
illw eavel ni hreet aysd, nda eb oneg
orf neo onthm. ringB na xtrae airp
fo andalss.

aulP

God's Saving Grace

Who Am I?

I have several different names I can go by. To figure out who I am is not so easy—I can change form. I am a fallen angel, and my name means "adversary." You may have heard me called the devil.
Who am I?

Satan

sanctuary: A peaceful place used for worship or safety. Tabernacles, churches, temples, and sanctuaries all have been used as holy places where people could gather together to be near God.

Words to Know

1. When Paul spoke to the Romans, what did he say about the Spirit?

2. What does Paul say this means?

3. When a person suffers with Christ, what happens?

4. Why does Paul feel the suffering is worthwhile?

5. According to Paul, by what means are we saved?
   a. By hope
   b. By faith
   c. By charity
   d. All of the above

6. What did Paul ask the people to have?

7. What will happen when everyone loves God?

8. According to Paul, who is for us even when others are against us?
   a. The prophets
   b. The king
   c. God
   d. Paul

9. How did God show He was willing to give up everything for us?

10. Where does Paul say that Christ is sitting?
    a. Below the feet of God
    b. On the right hand of God
    c. On the left hand of God
    d. Above God

11. What could possibly separate us from the love of Christ?
    a. Persecution
    b. Famine
    c. The sword
    d. All of the above

12. Even if sorrows come, what will happen?

The Lord's Day

1. Peter says that he repeats someone else's words. Whose words are they?

2. What did these people call those who question the promise of the Savior's coming?
   a. The liars
   b. The scoffers
   c. The thieves
   d. The misguided

3. Why do these disbelievers refuse to accept the truth?

4. Which event did Peter remind them of, that changed so many things in the past?
   a. The drought
   b. The volcano
   c. The flood
   d. The famine

5. According to Peter, what is the same as 1,000 years to the Lord?
   a. One day   c. One month
   b. One week   d. One year

6. How is it said that the Lord will come?

7. When that day comes, what is said to happen?

8. What does Peter suggest that people should do before these things come to pass?

9. How will the people of the future be different?

10. Since this is going to happen, how should people want to be known?
    a. At peace with Him
    b. Spotless
    c. Blameless
    d. All of the above

prophecy: A type of foretelling or prediction. Divine messages about the future were sent by God in the Bible through prophecy. These messages were usually delivered by prophets.

Words to Know

What is it that Adam never saw or had, yet left two of them for his children?

Parents!

An Angel with a Scroll

revelation: When something becomes known. In the Bible, God's message is revealed to men. Revelations may have something to do with the future, our values, or God himself.

Words to Know

1. These revelations were received by John, and they tell of a mighty angel. Where did the angel come from?

2. What elements from the skies are used to describe the angel?
   a. A cloud
   b. A rainbow
   c. The sun
   d. All of the above

3. The angel was holding something—what was it?
   a. The world
   b. The Lamb of God
   c. A lantern
   d. A little book or scroll

4. Where were the angel's feet?

A Lucky Number

The number seven appears frequently in the Bible. God created the world in seven days, and there were seven trumpets playing while seven priests marched seven times around the walls of Jericho. Another number that appears often is forty—the Israelites spent forty years in the wilderness; Jesus spent forty days in the desert. Can you think of other instances where this number appears?

5. What did his voice sound like?

6. Then he lifted something toward Heaven. Do you know what it was?
   a. His face
   b. The scroll
   c. His hand
   d. His wings

7. How did the angel describe God?

8. What did he say about the future?

9. When the sound of the seventh angel begins, what will happen?

10. What did the voice from Heaven command the writer to do?

11. When he had the book, what did the angel tell him?
    a. To eat it
    b. That the book was sweet like honey
    c. That the book would make his belly sour
    d. All of the above

12. Then what did the angel tell him to do?

A New Land

1. Why did John talk of a new Heaven and Earth?

2. What did he see coming down from God?
   a. A star
   b. The Holy City, a new Jerusalem
   c. A large cloud of dust
   d. Heavenly grace

3. Where did the voice from Heaven say God's dwelling would be?

4. When God wipes away the tears from their eyes, what will be no more?
   a. Crying
   b. Pain
   c. Death
   d. All of the above

5. The man who sat on the throne said he was the Alpha and the Omega. What does this mean?

6. Will the people be able to drink from the spring that holds the water of life?

7. Where did the angel take John to view the holy city?
   a. Into a cloud
   b. Onto his wing
   c. Up to the tallest tower
   d. Onto a high mountain

8. The walls of the Holy City were different—in what way?

9. Which type of metal was used to build the city and pave its streets?
   a. Gold
   b. Silver
   c. Brass
   d. All of the above

10. Why was there no temple in the city?

11. There was also no need for the sun or moon—do you know why?

Why did Eve want to move to New York?

She wanted to be near the Big Apple!

TRY THIS

▶ **Sand Dollar Stars**

Have you ever looked closely at a sand dollar? If you find one you can study, you will see the front has a star similar to the star that shone over Bethlehem. On the back there is a shape like an Easter lily. If you are allowed to break it open, you will see what look like doves.

The Return

Words to Know

1. What was coming out of the throne in the Holy City?

2. There was also the tree of life. What did the tree provide?
   a. Twelve different kinds of fruit
   b. Leaves that could heal
   c. A monthly harvest
   d. All of the above

3. What good thing will happen in the city?

4. Who did God send to say all of these things to John?
   a. An apostle
   b. An angel
   c. A prophet
   d. All of the above

5. What did the angel say would happen to those who obeyed the sayings of the prophecy?

6. Why did the angel say John should not worship at his feet?

7. The Lord says He is "coming soon." How will He decide what the people's reward should be?

8. Who does Jesus say he is?
   a. The Offspring of David
   b. The Root
   c. The bright Morning Star
   d. All of the above

9. If anyone adds to the words of the book, what will happen?
   a. He will see plagues
   b. He will see fire
   c. He will wander in the desert
   d. He will cry

10. What will happen to the one who takes away any part of the words?

11. How does the last promise of Jesus read?

What's in Your Future?

The Bible speaks of fortunetellers, or those who see the future. Some fortunetellers claim they can see the future while others only want to predict or guess at it. Some ancient fortunetellers used oil on water or chickens pecking at corn to see what the future held.

Fun Fact

Face Facts

Body Language is using actions, motions, or expressions—not words—to show how you feel. For example, crossed arms and a frowning face tell you that someone is upset. Many times in the Bible, people seemed to know something was wrong before anyone spoke. They also could tell when someone had changed by "reading" the expression on their face.

In this puzzle, you must first unscramble the letters in each box to form the name of a familiar emotion. Then, use a pencil or marker to draw the quickest path from each word to the face that shows that emotion! But be careful—paths can't cross over each other, and you can't cut through one face to get to another!

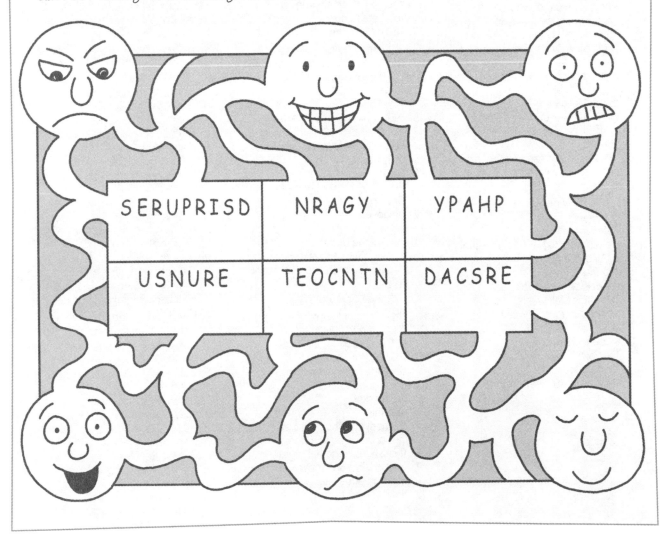

SERUPRISD	NRAGY	YPAHP
USNURE	TEOCNTN	DACSRE

Chapter 10 Answer Key

The Cross
1. "My kingdom is not of this world"
2. c. Barabbas
3. b. Thorns
4. c. The cross
5. c. The place of the skull
6. "Jesus of Nazareth, the King of the Jews"
7. They cast lots
8. d. All of the above
9. With the disciples
10. That he would return

The Resurrection
1. The stone that covered its entrance was rolled away
2. They have taken away the Lord
3. They did not know the scripture had said that he would rise again
4. Two angels
5. Not to hold him
6. a. The disciples
7. c. The Holy Spirit
8. He would have to see Jesus for himself
9. Thomas
10. "Blessed are those who have not seen me and yet have believed"
11. d. Bread and fish

Peter's Escape
1. d. James
2. Peter
3. He planned to hold a public trial
4. d. All of the above
5. An angel
6. He helped Peter wake up
7. The chains fell off his wrists
8. No, he thought he was having a vision
9. It opened by itself
10. The Lord
11. To the disciples
12. He was struck down and died

A Message from Paul
1. He was teaching the history of the Jews and preaching the Word of God
2. a. Many people came to hear him
3. The Jews were not honoring his message
4. To bring salvation to the ends of the Earth
5. On the Sabbath
6. He sailed
7. "Opened the doors of faith for the Gentiles"
8. Yes, to make the Gentiles a people of God's name
9. d. All of the above
10. Yes, it strengthened it

God's Saving Grace
1. The Spirit shows that we are children of God
2. We are heirs of God and co-heirs with Christ
3. That person also shares in Christ's glory
4. Because the glory is even better
5. a. By hope
6. Patience
7. We will be justified and glorified
8. God
9. He gave His son to save us
10. b. On the right hand of God
11. d. All of the above
12. We will always have "the love of God that is in Christ Jesus our Lord"

The Lord's Day
1. The words of the prophets, and of the Lord and Savior
2. b. The scoffers
3. They say that nothing has changed since the beginning of time
4. c. The flood
5. a. One day
6. As a thief
7. The heavens shall pass away and the Earth will be laid bare
8. They should lead holy lives
9. They will live on a new Earth filled with righteousness
10. d. All of the above

An Angel with a Scroll
1. Heaven
2. d. All of the above
3. d. A little book or scroll
4. His right foot was upon the sea and his left foot was on the Earth
5. The roar of a lion and the boom of thunder
6. c. His hand
7. As the eternal creator of all of Heaven and Earth
8. "There will be no more delay"
9. The mystery of God should be finished
10. To take the scroll from the hand of the angel
11. d. All of the above
12. To be a prophet again before all the peoples, nations, languages, and kings

A New Land
1. Because the old ones had passed away
2. b. The Holy City, a new Jerusalem
3. With men
4. d. All of the above
5. The Beginning and the End
6. Yes
7. d. Onto a high mountain
8. They were decorated and had the names of the twelve tribes of Israel written on them
9. a. Gold
10. The Lord God Almighty and the Lamb are its temple
11. Because the glory of God and the Lamb would provide the light

The Return
1. A river flowing with the water of life
2. d. All of the above
3. The people will see God's face
4. b. An angel
5. They would be blessed
6. They were equal
7. He will judge according to the work each one has done
8. d. All of the above
9. a. He will see plagues
10. His promise of the Holy City will be taken away
11. "The grace of the Lord Jesus be with God's people. Amen."

Appendix A
Books to Read

Beers, V. Gilbert. *Early Readers Bible.* Zondervan, 2001.

Bostrom, Kathleen Long. *What About Heaven?* Tyndale House Pub., 2000.

Carlson, Melody. *Don't Worry about Tomorrow: Just Like Jesus Said.* Broadman & Holman Publishers, 2002.

Gold, August, and Matthew J. Perlman. *Where Does God Live?* Skylight Paths Pub., 2001.

Goody, Wendy, and Veronica Kelly. *A Peek into My Church.* Whippersnapper Books, 1999.

Hample, Stuart. *Children's Letters to God.* Workman Publishing Company, 1991.

Henley, Karyn, and Dennas Davis. *The Beginner's Bible.* Zondervan Publishing Company, 1997.

Loth, Paul J. *My First Study Bible.* Tommy Nelson, 1994.

Mandali, Monique. *Everyone's Mandala Coloring Book: Volume 2.* Falcon Publishing Company, 1994.

Miralles, Joseph (illustrator). *Golden Children's Bible: The Old Testament and the New Testament.* Golden Books Pub Co Inc., 1999.

Partner, Daniel. *365 Read-Aloud Bedtime Bible Stories.* Spring Arbor Distributors, 1993.

Paydos, Michael. *The Everything® Bible Stories Book.* Adams Media, 2002.

Rock, Lois. *The Ten Commandments for Children.* Chariot Victor Pub., 2000.

Sose, Bonnie, and Holly Sose. *Designed by God So I Must Be Special.* Character Builders, 1990.

Spier, Peter. *Noah's Ark.* Picture Yearling, 1992.

Suggs, Rob. *The Comic Book Bible.* Barbour Co, 1997.

Zalben, Jane Breskin. *Let There Be Light: Poems and Prayers for Repairing the World.* Dutton Books, 2002.

Zondervan Adventure Bible NIV. Zondervan, 2000.

Zwerger, Lisbeth. *Stories from the Bible.* North South Books, 2002.

Appendix B
Bible Trivia Online

✎ *www.antelope-ebooks.com/CCC* Looking for poems, lessons, stories from the Bible, and tons of activities? This is the site for you!

✎ *www.childrensbiblestudy.com* This site includes several animated stories and resources for kids and adults alike.

✎ *www.faithfirst.com/html/kidClub/kidClub.asp* This is a jam-packed site containing songs, games, brain teasers, stories, and information about the saints.

✎ *www.fbg-church.org/coloring-book.htm* Check out this site's coloring book pages—all you have to do is print and then color.

✎ *www.gospelcom.net/cbh* If you are looking for Daily Devotions, Bible studies, or Bible trivia, this is the site for you!

✎ *www.kidsbible.com* At *kidsbible.com* you will meet two new friends by the names of Skweek and Tagg. Together you can play games, read passages, answer trivia, and try to help Jesus walk across the water.

✎ *www.mssscrafts.com* Crafts, coloring pages, and more are available for kids and Sunday school teachers at this resourceful site.

✎ *www.virtualchurch.org/kids.htm* For those of you who love to color, this site offers pictures from the Bible that you can print and color yourself. It also includes links to other fun sites.

✎ *www.whatagod.com/kidstrivia1.htm* Test your trivia skill with these five questions about the Bible and a couple of prayers.

Appendix C
Bible Glossary

anoint: The Bible tells of people who were anointed—marked with special oil. This sacred practice was used after bathing, for religious ceremonies, and for the appointment of people to positions of importance.

ark: A ship or boat used for travel on water. Moses' basket was called an ark. The same name was also given to the boat that Noah made before the flood.

Bible: The Bible is the Word of God that is held sacred in Christianity and Judaism. In this book you will find psalms, songs, history, and rules created to teach man about life in the past, present, and future.

birthright: In the days of the Bible it allowed the oldest son to inherit or receive everything that his father had. Some places in the world today still practice or honor the birthright.

blessing: The Lord gave His blessing to many of the people in the Bible. They were blessed with children, food, and happiness. Parents also gave their blessings or good wishes to their children. Today, people continue to use blessings in their daily lives.

burden: A weight or responsibility one must carry or bear. Jesus had the burden of carrying his cross and the sins of the people of the world.

cherubim: Small, childlike angels with wings. There are cherubim that guard the gates of Eden and the Ark of the Covenant. They could also be seen in several places throughout the tabernacles.

commandment: A rule, order, or law, such as the Ten Commandments that Moses received from God at Mount Sinai.

covenant: A promise or agreement between people or with God. God made many covenants or promises in the Bible. The rainbow was one of them.

decree: An order or decision given by a judge. There were many people who were judges in the Bible. Moses was one of the more famous ones.

elder: An older person with authority, or an official representing a group or organization. In the Bible, the elders were the religious leaders of their tribes. They were responsible for many of the tasks and decisions in the work of God.

forgiveness: The act of excusing or forgiving another person's weaknesses or errors. God speaks in the Bible of forgiving or pardoning the sins of His followers.

God: In the Bible, God is the creator of man and the Earth. Some Christians believe in the Holy Trinity of God the Father, God the Son, and God the Holy Spirit. Most religions worship an eternal God or ruler of the universe.

Hebrew: The Hebrews were the descendants of Abraham. They are mentioned throughout the Bible as the ones chosen by God. Hebrew is also the name given to their language. Today, modern Hebrew is the official language of Israel.

holy: To be holy is to be of a divine or sacred nature. The Bible speaks of the Holy Place, the Holy Ghost, and the Holy Spirit. All that is holy in the Bible is good and of God.

idol: A sacred or holy image or likeness that is shaped to look like a god. Many of the idols of the past were made of metal, such as gold. Contemporary idols are commonly made of ceramic or stone.

judge: To decide or assess a problem. A judge must choose between two or more sides to make a final decision. In the Bible, God judges many people by their hearts and their actions.

oath: An oath is a loyal vow or pledge. Giving an oath is one way to give someone your word or promise. God shared many oaths and vows with people in the Bible.

plague: An illness spread throughout a group of people, a terrible disaster, or problem. Many of the plagues mentioned in the Bible involve insects, animals, and nature.

prophecy: A type of foretelling or prediction. Divine messages about the future were sent by God in the Bible through prophecy. These messages were usually delivered by prophets.

prophet: Someone who foretells the future. There are many prophets in the Bible who receive signs from God and share them with other people.

religion: A belief in the creator of the universe. It is also a study or practice of faith in a god and the rules given to man. There are many different religions or faiths in our world.

repent: To feel sorrow or remorse for what you have done. To ask for forgiveness and say you are sorry are ways to repent. God wanted His followers to repent for their bad behavior.

revelation: When something becomes known. In the Bible, God's message is revealed to men. Revelations may have something to do with the future, our values, or God himself.

sacrifice: To sacrifice something, you must give it up. In Biblical times, people offered sacrifices to God to show Him their love and commitment. God sacrificed His son to show His love and fulfill the prophecy.

sanctuary: A peaceful place used for worship or safety. Tabernacles, churches, temples, and sanctuaries all have been used as holy places where people could gather together to be near God.

spirit: The energy or essence of a person or being. The Spirit of God is mentioned throughout the Bible. One part of God is the Holy Spirit, which fills the followers of God.

tribe: A group or band of people who share the same family ties. In the Bible, the tribes were given roles or jobs to do. For example, the tribe of Levi (the Levites) were the keepers of the temples and the tabernacles.

Puzzle Answers

page 3 • **Amazing Creation**

page 7 • **Find the Snake**

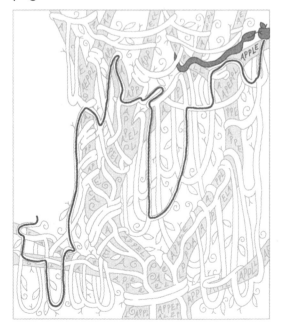

page 11 • **Happy Father's Day**

The three missing letters are A, S, and C.

A D A M 13 25 73 19	**130**	
Adam was the father of S E T H 27 19 32 27	**105**	
Seth was the father of E N O S H 9 53 12 3 13	**90**	
Enosh was the father of K E N A N 5 37 17 6 5	**70**	
Kenan was the father of M A H A L A L E L 12 3 4 10 12 13 3 1 7	**65**	

Mahalalel was the father of J A R E D 30 31 30 31 40	**162**
Jared was the father of E N O C H 13 13 13 13 13	**65**
Enoch was the father of M E T H U S E L A H 15 9 8 7 9 8 7 9 8 7	**87**
Methuselah was the father of L A M E C H 33 22 44 11 55 17	**182**
Lamech was the father of N O A H 125 100 125 150	**500**

pages 16–17 • **Two by Two**

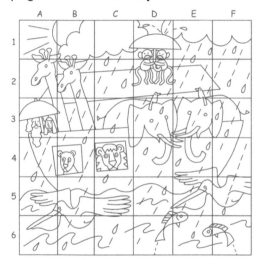

page 21 • **A Beautiful Promise**

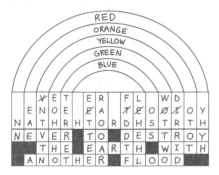

Puzzle Answers

page 26 • Camel Count

10 camels went to Mesopotamia.

page 29 • Tag the Twins

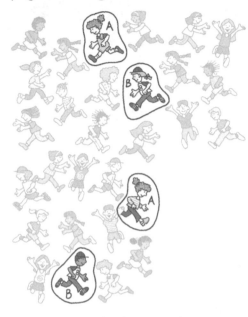

page 35 • Baby in a Basket

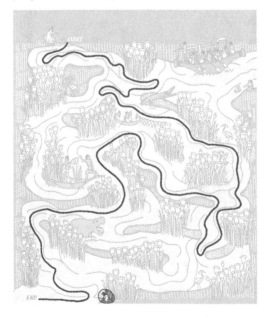

page 38 • Name Game

I DREW HIM OUT OF THE WATER

page 42 • Frogs Underfoot!

TOAD-ALLY AWFUL!

page 46 • The Rock of Horeb

page 52 • Guiding Angel

Puzzle Answers

page 56 • **Gifts from the Trees**

NANBAA
BANANA

CEPAH
PEACH

EPAPL
APPLE

UPLM
PLUM

GNORAE
ORANGE

YRECHR
CHERRY

REPA
PEAR

page 59 • **Stones from the River**

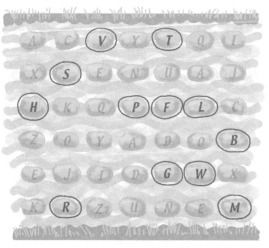

page 64 • **Strong Samson, Weak Samson**

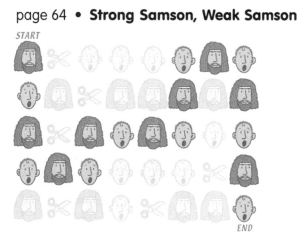

page 68 • **The Big Battle**

page 71 • **Where's Elijah?**

Turn the book one quarter turn counterclockwise, and you will see the prophet's face.

page 77 • **Room Service**

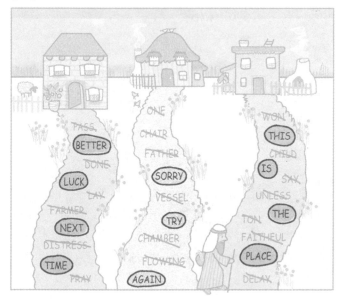

Puzzle Answers

page 78 • It's Official

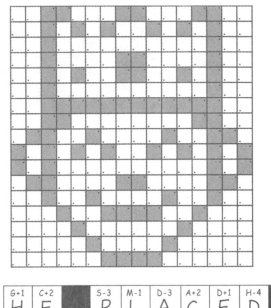

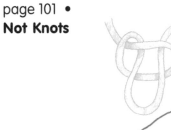

HE PLACED A CROWN ON HIS HEAD

page 85 • Royal Raft

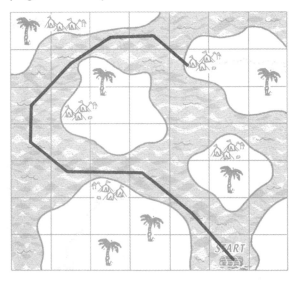

page 91 • The Golden Rule

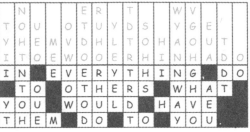

IN EVERYTHING, DO TO OTHERS WHAT YOU WOULD HAVE THEM DO TO YOU.

page 94 • Building in Jerusalem

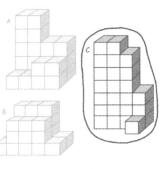

page 96 • Where's the Star?

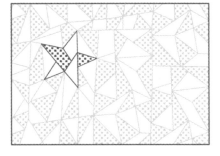

page 101 • Not Knots

Puzzle Answers

page 104 • **Food for 5,000**

page 110 • **Transformers**

Every kid will draw creatures that look completely different!

page 114 • **Cross Codes**

The place where the soldiers took Jesus to be crucified:

G O L G O T H A

This is what the name means:

ETH _THE_
EACPL _PLACE_
FO _OF_
HET _THE_
KULSL _SKULL_

page 117 • **Paul's Message**

Greetings!

Let us visit our brothers in every city where we have preached the word of the Lord and see how they are. We will leave in three days, and be gone for one month. Bring an extra pair of sandals.

Paul

page 123 • **Face Facts**

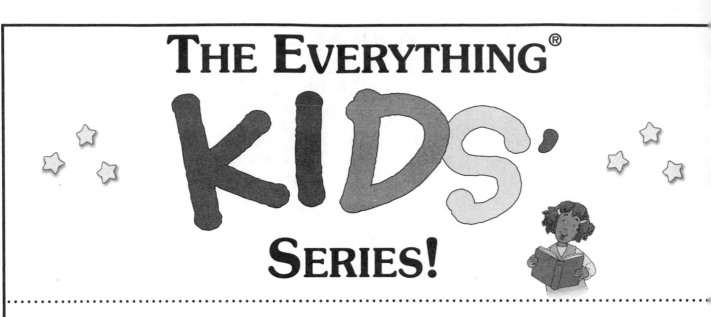

THE EVERYTHING® KIDS' SERIES!

Packed with tons of information, activities, and puzzles, the Everything® Kids' books are perennial bestsellers that keep kids active and engaged. Each book is 8" x 9¼", 144 pages, and two-color throughout.

All this at the incredible price of $6.95!

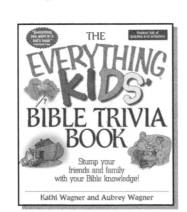

The Everything® Kids' Bible Trivia Book
1-59337-031-8

The Everything® Kids' Riddles & Brain Teasers Book
1-59337-036-9

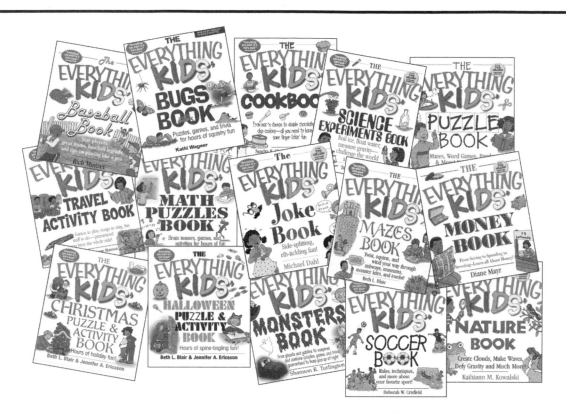

The Everything® Kids' Baseball Book, 3rd Ed.
UPDATED FOR SPRING 2004!
1-59337-070-9

The Everything® Kids' Bugs Book
1-58062-892-3

The Everything® Kids' Christmas Puzzle &
Activity Book 1-58062-965-2

The Everything® Kids' Cookbook
1-58062-658-0

The Everything® Kids' Halloween Puzzle &
Activity Book 1-58062-959-8

The Everything® Kids' Joke Book
1-58062-686-6

The Everything® Kids' Math Puzzles Book
1-58062-773-0

The Everything® Kids' Monsters Book
1-58062-657-2

The Everything® Kids' Mazes Book
1-58062-558-4

The Everything® Kids' Money Book
1-58062-685-8 ($11.95 CAN)

The Everything® Kids' Nature Book
1-58062-684-X ($11.95 CAN)

The Everything® Kids' Puzzle Book
1-58062-687-4

The Everything® Kids' Science Experiments Book
1-58062-557-6

The Everything® Kids' Soccer Book
1-58062-642-4

The Everything® Kids' Travel Activity Book
1-58062-641-6

All Kids' titles are priced at $6.95 ($10.95 CAN) unless otherwise noted.

Trade Paperback, $14.95
1-58062-147-3, 304 pages

The Everything® Bedtime Story Book

by Mark Binder

The Everything® Bedtime Story Book is a wonderfully original collection of 100 stories that will delight the entire family. Accompanied by charming illustrations, the stories included are retold in an exceptionally amusing style and are perfect for reading aloud. From familiar nursery rhymes to condensed American classics, this collection promises to promote sweet dreams, active imaginations, and quality family time.

The Everything® Mother Goose Book

by June Rifkin

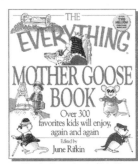

The Everything® Mother Goose Book is a delightful collection of 300 nursery rhymes that will entertain adults and children alike. These wonderful rhymes are easy for even young readers to enjoy—and great for reading aloud. Each page is decorated with captivating drawings of beloved characters. Ideal for any age, *The Everything® Mother Goose Book* will inspire young readers and take parents on an enchanting trip down memory lane.

Trade Paperback, $12.95
1-58062-490-1, 304 pages

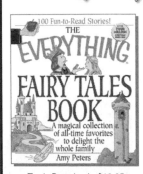

Trade Paperback, $12.95
1-58062-546-0, 304 pages

The Everything® Fairy Tales Book

by Amy Peters

Take your children to magical lands where animals talk, mythical creatures wander freely, and good and evil come in every imaginable form. You'll find all this and more in *The Everything® Fairy Tales Book*, an extensive collection of 100 classic fairy tales. This enchanting compilation features charming, original illustrations that guarantee creative imaginations and quality family time.